Inherited Illusions

Inherited Illusions

Integrating the Sacred and the Secular

THOMAS CULLINAN

Christian Classics, Inc.
P.O. BOX 30 · WESTMINSTER, MARYLAND
1988

First Published 1987 by Sheed and Ward, Ltd., 2 Creechurch Lane, London, England under the title, *THE PASSION OF POLITICAL LOVE.*

Nihil Obstat Anton Cowan, Censor.
Imprimatur Mgr. J. Crowley, V.G., Westminster, 20 August 1986.

ISBN: 0-87061-152-6

Printed in the United States of America

Acknowledgements

The author and publishers are grateful to the following for permission to quote from copyright works:

Abhishiktananda Society:
Saccidananda, by Abhishiktananda;

Faber & Faber Ltd:
Collected Poems 1909–1962, by T. S. Eliot;

S. C. M. Press Ltd:
Christianity Rediscovered, by Vincent Donovan.

Preface

DEAR READER,

This book was suggested by friends. It is made up of talks and essays spanning more than a decade. They have been left more or less in their original forms, so there are inevitable repetitions and outdated references. Much has happened, for instance, in the Philippines, since my reference to them.

Many years ago, when I was a sailor and our ship was in Rio de Janeiro, I made my way up to the huge statue of Christ on a pinnacle above the city. His right arm stretched out to the luxurious Atlantic hotels and dwellings of Copacabana beach, his left arm stretched out to the many thousands of shanty dwellers clinging to the hillsides inland. I pondered then, as I still do, what it meant to stand at his feet.

It is a passionate and political affair to be 'in Christ'.

THOMAS CULLINAN
Liverpool, October 1986

Contents

Inherited Illusions

CHAPTER ONE

The Passion of Political Love

TITLES which are obscure have their own advantages. Clear titles produce clear expectations, and then you have to fulfil those expectations. I want to write, surprisingly and perhaps obscurely, about *obedience*. I know that sounds a bit like an abbot's chapter, but it is very difficult to read the gospels and not take seriously the question of obedience. It was primary in what Jesus was preaching and in his own self-understanding.

The word *obedience* means, in its origins, being a good listener. And that connects with so much in the gospel about watching, being sensitive to the signs of the times, and to what the Spirit is saying to the churches—be an attentive listener. So the opposite of obedience, in the Latin origins of these words, is, believe it or not, *absurdity*, being utterly deaf. So we have only two options, perhaps ultimate options, in life: we are obedient or we are absurd.

Often in churchy circles, especially those of religious and monastic life, we have thought of obedience as having only one meaning: doing what you are told to do. There was not much reference to listening, to watching and praying. But it is dangerous to read the gospels with that limited idea of obedience in mind. For Jesus obedience was neither a static nor a regimenting thing; it was constantly evolving and deepening in its demands. That's what I want to talk about.

Obedience is not in fact simply listening nor simply doing what one is told to do. Obedience is the practical art of submitting self-interest to the demands of reality and truth, insofar as these are perceived. In that sense it is a basic call on every person, because every person is called to transcend the self-enclosing demands of the ego and the self-interesting drives of indulgence, in order to respond rationally and lovingly to the reality of the world at large and especially that of people. The paradox of the person is that one becomes fully human and free not by self-mindfulness but by self-forgetfulness in communion. Love is not a nice extra to being human, but its essence.

Clearly such obedience requires both the art of listening, pondering, watching (without which there is no perception of truth except as a projection of personal prejudice) and also the art of practical discretion, as to how to respond in fact and not just in wishful thinking.

Two basic calls of this universal obedience are that of the 'common good' and that of 'natural law'. The former is the practical art of assessing one's activities and pursuits in the context of the common good, or the social whole. If that obedience is ignored one is trapped by the plausible illusions of one's own family, or class, or nation or whatever. The latter – that of natural law – is the call to accept the nature of things, to live non-violently within the rhythms and characteristics of the material and human world. We have almost lost a feeling for this obedience because of our aggressive use of technology, and because of our pride at having 'come of age' – our modern insolence in assuming we can do what we like and how we like. We play God and call it freedom.

There are of course many other aspects of obedience. Anyone in vows, such as baptism or marriage or religious life, freely embraces specific forms of obedience which characterise that way of life – in baptism to the Word of God and the community of faith, in marriage to one's spouse and family, in religious life to a community and a superior. But it is sad that obedience has had a bad press in recent times, when it is so central to the whole New Testament understanding of the human person, of community, and of liberation.

Obedience In Jesus

1. The Obedience of Belonging

The first obedience in the life of Jesus was that which carried him to the age of about thirty. We need not dwell on it, partly because the church and our institutions have dwelt on this sort of obedience long enough, though the gospels hardly do so at all. In fact we have very little evidence about that period of Jesus' life, except that he emerged at the age of thirty as the son of a carpenter, somebody who as far as we know obeyed all the norms of religious and cultural expectations. One of the difficulties that the people of Nazareth had about Jesus was precisely that he was so normal until that age. And you know the feeling when one of our own members, one of our own family or community, suddenly gets up and is different from us, we wonder what on earth right they have to be holier or more truthful or more far seeing than we are. After all we all come from the same slot. That early obedience I am calling the *obedience of belonging* and it has been important in each of our lives in nurturing us in faith.

2. The Obedience of Truth for Communion

At some stage we know nothing about, before his baptism, Jesus made that extraordinary decision to set forth from the odd-job man's bench into the highways and byways of Galilee and proclaim the kingdom. I am going to call this obedience, which evolved after his baptism and the temptation in the desert, *the obedience of truth for communion.* (I had thought of calling it the obedience of political love, which may be as good.) Why? Jesus came forth preaching and proclaiming a kingdom of God among people. Not simply as the prophets had done, something that was in the future, but something that was being realised in his own person and in his presence, something definitive. This kingdom was not simply a conversion of hearts, it wasn't simply a spiritual renewal, in a pleasant pastoral, romantic, place of peasants and fishermen. The scene in which Jesus proclaimed the kingdom was far more like the scene in El Salvador or Northern Ireland or South Africa today than it was like Ambridge or some rural part of Ireland.

One of the great blessings we enjoy today is that we have more resources of scriptural studies and scriptural understanding than the church has ever had, perhaps since Pentecost. We probably know more about scripture today than the church has ever known in her history. That is a remarkable blessing from God. And one of the things this has helped us understand is that Jesus came into a scene that was highly politically conscious. And he wasn't saying, as most of us picked up in our childhood, he wasn't saying: abandon all that murky political side of life, enter into a private spiritual renewal of heart and everything else will look after itself. The people he was amongst were living under the heavy dominance of moneylenders and tax collectors. They were acutely aware of the domination of the Roman authorities, and Jesus in his youth would have seen people crucified by the road after summary arrest. The Roman authorities were very like many of the worst repressive regimes we know today and they had a particular line about the Jews. And Jesus arrived in this scene preaching a kingdom that was thoroughly incarnational. He was coping with real issues of daily life.

By the time the gospels were written the interest of the early Christians had shifted. They were in a different situation and some of the reporting of what Jesus had said had already been adapted. A small example of that is: 'Forgive us our debts as we forgive those who are indebted to us.' That was to do with money, but by the time it comes into the Our Father we inherit it as to do with sins and peccadillos. When St Paul says 'Be indebted to no one' he's not talking simply about spiritual sins, although it has that reference. He is talking about concrete ways of living life in a liberated way.

The jubilee year, or the year of the Lord's favour, was held every fifty years. It was intended as a year in which to become aware of creeping injustice and to restore

God's justice in the affairs of life. Its main demands, however much they may have been dodged in practice, were to restore the land by leaving it fallow, to set free those oppressed by indebtedness, to liberate slaves, and to re-distribute capital (and land). It was all about ecological and political love.

There may have been a jubilee year about the time Jesus began preaching, in AD 26/27. Certainly it was a dramatic moment in the synagogue at Nazareth when he read Isaiah 61. 1–2, concluding with its reference to 'the year of the Lord's favour', closed the book and said, 'Today this is realised . . . ' There are references, especially in the Sermon on the Mount, to the fundamental demands of the jubilee year. (See *The Politics of Jesus* by John Howard Yoder, ch. 3.)

The jubilee year was meant to anticipate into the present the great Shalom, the great sabbath, of God's final kingdom. This is perhaps what we mean by saying that the life of the church is to be a sacrament of God's kingdom, the realised unity of all the world in God's love. We are called to anticipate that kingdom into the concrete affairs of today to allow God to realise it fully through history. God's will on earth as in heaven.

One of the scandalous things that Jesus was doing in proclaiming this kingdom was laying bare the nature of the injustice and oppression in that society and, much to the dislike of many of his contemporaries, he was not too interested in the Roman domination. What he was preaching to the people was that the enemies of a nation are within itself, the internal oppressions and domination, for instance, between the authorities in the capital and the outsiders in Galilee, who were a despised group for the officials in

Jerusalem. Jesus was saying that those internal oppressions among the people themselves were the key issues in a pending catastrophe. He was warning them that fidelity to the kingdom of God and the relationships of justice amongst themselves would be the crucial issue in which the people would find salvation or collapse. Hence so many of his urgent warnings, and a sort of pathos, towards the end as the crucifixion approached.

For Jesus justice was thoroughly rooted in the whole scriptural tradition of the prophets and the psalms. (One of the excellent things about our liturgy moving from Latin into English is that it is now impossible for us to say the office daily or attend to readings at mass without becoming aware of issues of justice that we could otherwise forget.) Jesus' entire mind was formed by the tradition of scripture: the way he thought, the way he interpreted life, the way he interpreted God amongst people. But justice in scripture is not, as so much of our contemporary approach understands it, a question of egalitarianism. It wasn't a question of fairness.

God is not 'fair', and so many of the parables remind us of that. Justice in scripture is fundamentally based on community or bringing into the communion of social life and culture and religion, which were all the same for the Jewish mind, those who are excluded—excluded because they are either treated as sinners or because they are lepers or because they are Samaritans or because they are unlearned in the law or for any reason at all. Justice is a question of bringing in those who are being excluded and its root and origin is that if God is God and is One, then his people cannot be divided without blaspheming the God who formed them into a people. So that to know God and to live his presence among us is precisely to bring in those who are excluded. The scandal, for instance, of the rich in the gospels is not that they are well off and others are poor and if only everyone could be equally well off then everything would be all right. (That is the basic attitude and language of much of our contemporary approach. The Brandt Report for instance. If only everyone can get on the bandwagon, then we will have justice.) The scandal of the rich in the gospel is that their very wealth gave them a false security and a false little world of their own which was essentially divisive, and the only way out of that is to face the problems of the rich, not simply try and solve the problems of the poor.

Now the proclamation of the kingdom, as you know from the gospels, led not to the glorious welcome of life and community that one might expect—it led to misunderstanding; it led to confrontation. There is a brief reference in Mark 3 which hints at the pathos of this: Jesus' own family seem to have thought he had gone mad. Translate that into your own family life and you can get a feel for the growing suffering and solitude of the prophetic proclamation that was in Jesus. As the story proceeded the buoyancy of the early proclamation, the buoyancy of choosing the apostles and sending them to proclaim the good news amongst people, dwindles. We can sense this change of key, reading the gospels. It simply isn't working and the crucial question arises: when truth doesn't take amongst people, when justice is rejected, what do we do? The solution that most of us would come to is to muster more forces, to choose more apostles, to bring in the bigger guns and to force in that which is not being understood. For Jesus the option was other and the turning-point seems to have come when instead of being a fairly withdrawn figure in the outskirts, he suddenly burst on to the public national scene. Possibly that occurred at the cleansing of the temple, which surely happened much earlier in the story than the synoptic gospels give it. It was a very significant moment.

Another significant moment which we read, sadly, as a rather charming pastoral scene, was the feeding of the 5,000 as we call it – probably an organised meeting to take Jesus and make him into a political figure. We can see the equivalent issues today when struggles for justice and communion in fascist countries lead only to greater oppression and division. Does one adopt the language and methods of power, wealth and manipulation, and if not, what is the way forward? The way forward for Jesus was to rely totally on the intrinsic truth of his message, and on the conviction that all people, in their heart, can recognise truth; that's why it becomes divisive. He went forward in the confrontation that could not but lead to suffering, to compassion, that is to suffer with and for people. I think today it is very important that we understand this side of the gospel. So my third obedience I am calling the obedience of truth in compassion. Compassion – to suffer with and for.

It is often underestimated in studies of the social and political aspects of Jesus' life how much that side of life depended on his prayer, his intimacy with his Father, and the guidance of the Spirit. Indeed it was only that intimacy, that inner assurance of the Spirit, which is able to lift political love from righteous forms of selfwill into a truly self-less compassion. Without that intimacy it is impossible to say 'I come to do, not my own will, but that of him who sends me'. And he was accused of being a self-appointed prophet.

In times of political and social ambiguity, especially times of heightened political consciousness, to perceive where truth lies presupposes the 'long leisure and diligent search' of which More speaks. Indeed it presupposes a real poverty of spirit. But it is only truth that sets us free in such situations, seeing beyond conforming expectations, and acting beyond the demands of 'fear or favour'.

In the end that which distinguishes the prophetic truth which is of God from that which comes from self or merely from ideology, is the readiness of the prophet to suffer and to die (though even that, apart from intimacy with God and true humility, can be a high-minded ego-centred martyrdom for the cause).

The threefold pattern of obedience—belonging, communion, passion—is found in the lives of many followers of Christ. It is very clear, for instance, in Paul, whose initial conversion from the 'belonging' expectations of the law into the freedom of Christ was precisely his mystical appreciation of the communion of Christians 'in Christ' and the incorporation of gentile outsiders. It was this realisation and the misunderstandings and confrontations it led to which caused him so much suffering. Is the pattern, possibly, one that is realised—with different nuances—in the lives of all who follow, who allow truth to set them free?

3. *The Obedience of Truth in Compassion*

I am going to omit the details of the story of this obedience because they are familiar. But in order to understand a little bit of what was happening in the last parts of Jesus' life, first listen to familiar words from Isaiah—words which we hear during the Holy Week liturgy—

> Surely he has borne our griefs and carried our sorrows; yet we esteemed him as stricken, smitten by God and afflicted. He was oppressed and he was afflicted, yet he opened not his mouth; like a lamb that is led to the slaughter, like a sheep that before its shearers is dumb, so he opened not his mouth. By oppression and judgement he was taken away; and as for his generation, who considered that he was cut off out of the land of the living, stricken for the transgression of my people? He shall divide the spoil with the strong; because he poured out his soul to death, and was numbered with the transgressors; yet he bore the sin of many and made intercession for the transgressors (Is 53).

Now the great question is of whom was Isaiah speaking?

The prophets by and large speak of two things at the same time. They speak of something that is present in their own society and they also refer to something that is to come in the future. There is a strange and rather mysterious double language being used. I believe that Isaiah was speaking in the first place of the affliction of his people in the captivity in Babylon. He was saying that the afflicted in society absorb in themselves, and in their affliction, the sin of that society as a whole. In our own day we might say that those who are unemployed or the blacks in our society or the homeless in our society absorb in their affliction the sin of our society as a whole. Now that's a very much wider and more demanding approach to sin that the privatised and spiritualised idea of sin that most of us have been brought up on and might mention in confession. But it's a very scriptural idea that a nation or society embodies its sin in the whole way it operates and deals with people and that the poor absorb that sin. Isaiah looks forward to the time when one would come who, through free option, through deliberate choice, and through becoming a voice for the afflicted, would take on himself, would absorb and carry that sin of society. And because he would do so totally freely and innocently and therefore totally lovingly, he would bear that sin away. What do we mean by bearing sin away?

There is something profound and totally unique to the Jewish-Christian tradition in understanding what was happening in this last part of Jesus' life and we cannot reduce it to anything other than understanding God's redemption in and among his people.

Obedience In Us

It may be a little clearer now why I chose the mysterious title for this chapter, *The Passion of Political Love,* because what tends to happen—what happened in the life of Jesus and what I suspect has happened in the lives of most people—is this: one begins with an easy obedience and an easy love, however difficult our family or community relations may be; then through the action of God in us our love is expanded into a political love, a love of people within the social whole; and this then becomes a wounded solitude, a lived passion, a death.

Now in the New Testament the primary imperative on the Christian was to follow Jesus. It appears again and again through the gospels and the epistles. And 'to follow Jesus' didn't mean any simple 'imitation of Jesus'. For instance he was celibate. But when Paul was defending his own celibacy, it never even crossed his mind that he ought to be celibate because Jesus was. He doesn't argue it from that reason at all. Precisely what are the reasons for celibacy is a matter for discussion, but that's not what 'following Jesus' meant.

There are many other things that Jesus was and did and so on, but it didn't occur to them to put them under the title 'To Follow Jesus'. But what did come under the title 'To Follow Jesus', under that basic imperative, was precisely to take the same stance in society and toward people and toward the social whole that Jesus had, and to be led by it into an identification with the oppressed and the poor and the afflicted and to suffer as a result. So the same pattern if we are open to the same Spirit, dare I say the wounding Sword of the Spirit, as Jesus was, will carry us along the same path. The only mystery is why it ever came to be called the Good News.

1. The Obedience of Belonging

We begin with an obedience of belonging and for us the belonging that we had in our youth, as I mentioned, was a very private spiritualised idea of Christian faith. And I think if we are honest with ourselves this cannot cope with what has hit most of us who are present here in the last 10 or 20 years. It can't cope with interpreting the realities of our society. (It may be able to cope with devotions in the cathedral, but it cannot cope with what's across the yard in Victoria Street and that is part of our dilemma.)

2. The Obedience of Truth for Communion.

So we find ourselves carried by the grace of God into a love for people and for truth that goes beyond the bounds of domestic relationships.

As Jesus would say, if you only love those who love you within your families, so what? Even our pagan friends manage that sort of barter system. With you it is to be other. And if we make that option for the poor and the afflicted that the church and the scriptures ask us to make, then we must work and transform our whole awareness into that sense of truth for community and communion which is at the heart of Christian faith.

It is very difficult for the western mind to understand the authentic Christian faith in communion because we inherit a way of thinking about ourselves and one another and about man which is so private and so individual that we look on relationships as mere accidents. This is partly because Catholic scholastic theology described the human person as a 'first substance' and therefore all relationships were 'accidents', so that love for one another was a sort of resulting commandment which we ought to do as a moral duty but wasn't to do with the very nature of who we are. Even worse than that Catholic tradition is the Protestant misreading of the human person as the human individual and resulting total privatisation of life. And western philosophers, working, I suppose, from that Christian tradition, even if rejecting it, have brought us to a more and more private and isolated idea of who we are. Yet embedded in our real tradition and spoken to us most deeply by the mystics in our tradition is that the very heart of who we are, what we are as persons, is not an isolated and autonomous self, but is precisely communion.

If God is communion because of the Trinity, then the fundamental reality about ourselves is that we are communion, and therefore the basic drive in us – in spite of Freud and Adler and everybody else who has tried to locate the basic drive in us – the basic drive is to make real, to 'realise' that oneness which is what we are. In the words of Teilhard:

> Receive, O Lord, this all-embracing host which your whole creation, moved by your magnetism, offers you at this dawn of a new day. This bread, our toil, is of itself, I know, but an immense fragmentation; this wine, our pain, is no more, I know, than a draught that dissolves. Yet in the very depths of this formless mass you have implanted – and this I am sure of for I sense it – a desire, irresistible, hallowing, which makes us cry out, believer and unbeliever alike, 'Lord make us one' ['The Mass on the World', *Hymn of the Universe* (Fontana edition, p. 20)].

And that, I suggest to you, is the heart of concern for justice and for the poor. It is totally denied by the modern philosophy in a growing number of countries, of national security, which sees the nation as more important than its members. It lines up people as being either good or bad, as being either loyal or of the devil, and is the modern form of that ancient and all-pervasive heresy, the Manichaean heresy. It is probably the most evil thing in our world today. People are not dispensable. The Christian analysis of all creation and all society is not that some is good and some is evil, but that all is good, all is fallen and all is in need of redemption. So let us never divide either ourselves or society into those who are of God and those who are of the devil.

3. The Obedience of Truth in Compassion

The final obedience that this longing and working for community cannot but bring us to is the compassion and the suffering and, indeed, the death that each of us must take and absorb willingly into ourself on behalf of the afflicted. If we love those who suffer and are cast out, it cannot but lead to trouble, and the enemies we come up against will be within our own household, two divided against three and so on. This gospel is divisive. The mystery isn't that we don't have enemies; as Gustavo Gutierrez says: the mystery is that we should love our enemies, and we can't love them if we don't have them.

I would like to quote a passage from Jacques Maritain written many years ago which says something which I really want to share with you:

> Whenever we cope with the ingredients of human history we tend to look at things in terms of action, or ideas which lead to action. But we need to consider them also, and primarily, in terms of *existence.* I mean that there is a more fundamental order than that of political and social action: the order of *communion in life,* in aspirations and in suffering . . . *To act for* (people) belongs to the order of benevolence. But to *exist with* and *to suffer with* belongs to the order of love-in-unity . . . The person I love, I love right or wrong and I wish to exist and suffer with.

> *To exist with . . .* does not mean to live with someone in the geographical sense, nor to live in the same way; it does not mean loving merely in the sense of wishing someone well. It means loving a person in the sense of becoming one, of bearing the burdens, of living a common moral life, of feeling with and suffering with that person.
>
> If one loves that human thing we call 'the people' —which like all human and living things is, I know, difficult to define, and yet all the more real for that—if one loves the people, one's first and basic desire is to exist with, to stay in communion with, the people.
>
> Before doing them good, before working for their good, before accepting or rejecting the political line of this or that group claiming to support their interests, before carefully weighing up the good and evil expected of various doctrines and historical processes which seek their support, before choosing amongst these options or even rejecting them all, before doing any of these things, one would choose to exist with people, to suffer with them, to assume their hardships and their destiny [*The Range of Reason*, London, 1953, pp. 121 f].

Now most of us here find ourselves in the peculiar anguish of middle-class people whose consciousness and awareness have become sensitive to the affliction of the poor, while knowing there is nothing that any of us can do to identify and share in the memory and insecurity of the afflicted. People get worried about that, and especially people in religious orders, because a religious order is, in our modern society, one of the most secure ways of existing. (We won't go into that: full employment, square meals and no redundancy!) But I suggest that within that anguish there are ways in which God in his mercy and his kindness takes us into the suffering of Christ, the poor and the afflicted.

Once you really absorb into yourself a sense of communion with the poor, communion with the afflicted, knowing them as kith and kin with yourself, then life will never again be the same. You find yourself at various moments, occurring undesigned in life, being a voice for the voiceless, being ready to speak truth when it's awkward and it sounds absurd and it's ambiguous, and you finish up in some way a nonconformist, in some way slightly bonkers, in some way not fitting in. That can be real suffering and most of us in this room know what I am talking about. It happens for many people involved in, say, Justice and Peace work or in work for the homeless. It happens in local parishes where things used to make sense under an obedience of belonging, but now under the other obediences, seem to make us outsiders from that which nurtured us.

Another way I believe in which we must freely, even cheerfully, accept in ourselves the wound of compassionate love is when the demonic power of structures for oppression and injustice in our society flow down and around our awareness and seem to crush us, bringing a terrible dread that we are all involved in processes about which no one can do anything—that terrible sense of fate from which the whole gospel seeks to free us, but which at times we feel acutely—the sheer power mustered behind the injustice of our world. There is an easy way out of this agony—don't we know it—by adopting an over naive social analysis and indulging in some left-wingy righteousness. I'm not suggesting that analysis is invalid. I think it is essential—we need analysis and we must make political options—but it will not cope with a personal living out of the gospel and the cross of Christ. I think what I am suggesting is that we cannot indulge in being concerned for the afflicted but then shun suffering with and for them. It will affect every detail of our life—the way we live, the way we embrace poverty, the friends we have and the friends we lose, the form of security we seek to have, or not have, in life, the fundamental options we make about the sort of work we do and don't do. All things in life start to connect and I believe that is one of the signs, and thank God for it, that we are under an obedience and are the work of God's spirit and not simply on some ego trip, because that's our danger, is it not?

Naughtily—and I would not share this with many people I might talk to, but in this closed hall it's all right—naughtily I would like to finish by sharing, and slightly adapting, something Jim Forest wrote in the United States. I do so to remind us, myself especially, that if we are not under a true obedience and humility to God, if we do not act from an experience of the intimacy and the love of God as our Father, for ourselves and his people, then we will slide into forms of righteousness, which, however good they seem to be, will block the liberating work of God amongst us.

> Two men (they might have been women) went into a church to pray, one a radical and the other a conservative. And the radical looked straight at the altar, thinking, 'I thank you, God, that I am

not like that conservative over there: colour television, a new car, credit cards, children at a public school. I subscribe to the *New Internationalist,* I'm on the Justice & Peace Commission, I fast for CAFOD every Friday, I march against the National Front, I have an old black-and-white TV, I bake my own bread, and I read Hans Kung.' And the other man could hardly bear to look at the altar and he hung his head and prayed, 'Lord I am in a mess. Be merciful to me, a sinner' [Jim Forest, 'With Apologies to Luke', *National Catholic Reporter,* 10 August 1979].

CHAPTER TWO

Violence Within and Violence Without

DURING the last two weeks, as I pondered what to share with you tonight, I've had a growing feeling that the topic is far more important and far less manageable than I bargained for. I suggested the rather throw-away title; so the responsibility is mine. But I beg your indulgence if we journey at the edge of understanding. I ask you to come with me and travel in that hinterland.

In order to have a few pointers on our way, let me give six signposts before we set out, six headings to give a preview feeling for what we are doing:

1) Brief comment on the correspondence between the inner conflict within each of us, and the external social conflicts in our society.
2) Reflections on our inner conflicts, and a Christian understanding of them.
3) How the inner conflict affects the social conflict outside ourselves.
4) How the outer, social, conflict affects the inner.
5) The 'lock-on' between these two forms of conflict

—how we seem unable to escape from either of them because the other is there.

6) How do we break that lock-on hold?

1. Inner/Outer

So, our first part is the parallelism, the mirroring, the interconnectedness, between inner conflict in ourselves and the outer conflict in society. I would like to clarify this by thinking of three different ways in which we can read the Gospels and in particular the crisis in the Gospels—that confrontation between Jesus and the authorities ending in the Passion and the Crucifixion.

We can read the antagonism to Jesus as that of simply defined baddies, and the climax as the more or less inevitable outcome of the clash of social and political forces, ending in the death of Christ. The aggression present there and the violence are external to the reader. We read basically as a spectator, although we may of course start to identify with one side or the other. (And of course all of us know that we are on the side of the goodies, do we not?)

The second way of reading the Gospels, which fits more with our traditional piety, is to be unconcerned with political or social or historical forces present in the story and to read the climax of the Cross as a confrontation between my own personal sin and the goodness of God revealed in Jesus. Most of the writings of traditional piety have been that way of reading the Gospels.

The first way is that which nowadays we associate with liberation theology and political awareness in Latin America or wherever, and the second is the one that most of us have been brought up on. In the first one, we identify the crucified and the crucifiers in terms of particular people in society, the oppressed and the oppressors, and the invitation to us is to engage in political, social involvement. In the second one we recognise the crucified and the crucifier in ourself. There is in me both that which crucifies and that which is crucified; I become aware of both in myself as a I gaze on the crucified Christ. And I am called to a personal metanoia of my life, a personal liberation as a result of what I read in the Gospel.

Those are the first two ways of reading the Gospels. But what I want to suggest to you, and this is where I grope, is a further way of reading the Gospel, particularly its crisis in the Cross of Christ, in which we try to appreciate and understand the correspondence between the public, external, social conflict and the personal conflict in ourself. We try to appreciate that those two are not simply accidental, alongside, types of conflict, but that one feeds the other and the other feeds the one. And that it is possible for us to read in the Gospels both happening at the same time. This is quite important for us today for reasons we will come to later.

I recognise in the crucified one both the crucifier and the crucified in myself and the crucifiers and the crucified in society. And somehow it is by taking both very seriously that liberation is possible at both levels. (If that is obscure then at least you are with me.)

2. *Conflict within*

We are now going to look for a moment at the 'conflict within', inner conflict. I would like to start with a little story told by Krishnamurti.

'In the cool of one morning, God and the Devil walked together, as is their wont. And as they walked they noticed Man stoop down and pick out of the dust a grain of Truth. God nudged the Devil and said, "There, you see, he does recognise it when he sees it." "Yes", replied the Devil, "but give him time; he will organise it and then it will be mine." '

That story was undoubtedly told originally, and it no doubt delights our naughty ears, because of the modern lie that any organisation of truth hands it over to the Devil. The Devil is a liar, but he is always a plausible liar. This is why anti-Christ always looks so like Christ himself. On the other hand God cannot be a liar; he is always true, and he is right when he says (if that doesn't sound too condescending) that man can recognise what is true and what is good when he meets it. We are not simply made up of opinions, persuasions and views. Why do I say this and why is it so important?

It is because we have within us the image of the unseen God. That which Eastern writers call 'the true self' and indeed some Western psychiatrists. That which Scripture calls 'the heart' or 'the spirit'—that marvellous scriptural word that can never quite decide whether it should be spelt with a capital 's' or a small 's'. 'The Spirit led Jesus into the desert'. 'The Spirit speaks to our spirit words beyond understanding'. It is that in us which Hopkins calls 'the immortal diamond', hidden, waiting to be revealed. It is the meeting point, beyond the access of normal language, between the spirit of man and the spirit of God. 'I have said it, ye are gods'.

Every higher religion—Jewish, Christian, Hindu, Islam—must affirm and re-affirm this heart, this spirit, this self, as transcendent. And one thing we certainly mean by transcendent is that we are dealing with a reality which lies beyond the scope of normal, rational, daily language. Our transcendent self is accessible to the intuitions of the heart and of faith, but not to the normal language of daily experience. It is this transcendent self which the author of the *Cloud* calls our naked being; he invites us beyond the reaches of everyday language and experience when he writes:

> My dear friends in God, go beyond your intellect's endless and involved investigations and worship the Lord your God with your whole being. Offer him your very self in simple wholeness . . .
>
> If you analyse any or all of man's refined faculties and exalted qualities, you will come at length to the farthest reaches and ultimate frontiers of thought only to find yourself face to face with naked being itself . . . At first you might say 'I am, I see and feel that I am. And I possess all sorts of personal talents and gifts'. But after counting up all these in your mind, you could still go a step further . . . 'That which I am, and the way I am, with all my gifts of nature and grace, you have given to me, O Lord, *and you are all this.* I offer it all to you—principally to praise you, and also to help my fellows and myself' . . .
>
> You will find yourself, in the end, on the essential ground of being with a naked perception and blind awareness of your own being [The Book of Privy Counselling. Chap. 3].

To put this another way, our 'empirical' or 'conscious' self, aware of our daily behaviour, experiences, actions and reactions, has an articulate, indeed talkative language. It has words to talk about itself to ourselves and to others. But our transcendent self, where alone we are truly ourselves, and divine, has only the language of analogy and intuition (which is why, I suppose, people today have such a very low self-image: they can't believe they're divine if they can only accept what is empirical and immediate in their experience).

Now our problem of violence seems to start here. Our empirical self, which we have daily experience of and access to, is largely dominated by our 'ego'—that in us which holds us subservient to immediate vested interest, a slave to our prejudice, to security, to our passions and perhaps above all and embracing all the others, to fear. 'Fear not' was Jesus' constant command. The two things which Jesus repeated more than any other thing through the Gospel was the need to 'fear not' and to 'watch'. The two things that the ego holds us enslaved to are fear and blindness, brought on by the security of immediate vested interests.

My pilgrimage through life, our personal pilgrimages through life, into the freedom of God where we will know ourselves as totally free and indeed divine—this pilgrimage is precisely a bringing into harmony of my conscious self with my real self, the bringing into harmony of that which I consciously experience and know about with that which is real and ultimate and divine in me, my heart. It is somewhat like the bringing of a great orchestra into harmony with a composer. A process which always involves pain, always involves a loss of self-consciousness, but takes off into a sort of transcendent freedom which is simply not possible when the orchestra first meets for practice.

As long as my ego dominates my conscious self it will always set up this process of harmonisation as conflict. It is always going to present a conflict between what is real and ultimate on one hand and my immediate interests, fears and passions, on the other. And I suggest that this is where our inner conflict and our inner violence lies. But we have got to try and understand aright what it is.

As I lay in bed deciding that the first two drafts of what I have just been talking to you about were not even plausible lies but just wrong, I thought that the following was a possible way of putting it and I share it with you just as a sharing. You can hammer me down afterwards. This is it: if the heart of man is capable of recognising *truth,* my ego presents me with a plausible caricature of this in ever *seeking to be right.* Quite a different thing and yet near enough like the real thing to be plausible. And of course we all know, if we have any self knowledge, that our desire to be right, to prove ourselves right and to be proved right by others, really, in practice, works out as proving somebody else wrong. Therefore I must have enemies. I must have somebody around who I can prove to be wrong. And what I am suggesting is that this is a sort of caricature version going on of what is real in us, which is an ability to seek and recognise and love Truth.

Again if the heart of man is capable of recognising and seeking what is *good,* my ego presents me with a plausible caricature of this in ever seeking to *look good.* It is a sort of fool's version of the original.

Again the heart of man is capable of expanding bit by bit to a truly *cosmic love* and a *universal pity* (I do not mean a sort of impersonal pity, but a real love and a pity for people as people, not as 'my people'); my ego ever presents this in a plausible caricature version of *'looking after one's own'.* ('Charity begins at home' really denies all Jesus' preaching.) The ability I have because of my divinity—dare I say it—is towards a truly cosmic love as my Father in heaven loves, but I caricature this by looking after my own, my own people. Likewise, I have in me an infinite capacity for universal pity, but I caricature and stifle this by egocentric *self-pity*—setting up myself and my own as innocent victims of circumstances. Self-pity, that terrible illusion.

So the inner conflict in me is not between—and this cannot be said too often because of the perennial manichaean heresy that lies in the Church's history right down through 2,000 years and will go on for ever—the inner conflict in me is not between something in me which is good and something in me which is evil; it is not a conflict between soul and body, between spirit and matter. How can that be the conflict if Jesus presents us with himself as bread and wine? The conflict in us is not a manichaean dualism. The conflict in us is between our real, true, divine self and the caricature interests of our ego enslaving us to fear, prejudice and so on.

Why don't we simply resolve this thing by saying 'no' to ego and 'yes' to that which is true in us? The problem is one of language. Those of you who have ever sat on a committee know that if there are people on a committee who are articulate, clear, have plausible and immediate solutions to problems and come up with a nice programme which will start tomorrow and doesn't make too many demands on us, and that if they are arguing over against somebody who is tentative, perhaps much wiser, sees things in a much more ultimate light, but for that reason hasn't got a clear cut definite language or programme, then we all know who is going to carry the day on that committee.

I don't know whether any of you have watched it happen but I have, and one can forecast half an hour before the vote what is going to happen. Perhaps that is not just a parallel but perhaps it is the public version of the personal version of the same thing happening within each of us. The ego has clear-cut plausible immediate reasons for itself, and the intuitions of the heart, unless we learn to listen to them—and this is one of the gifts of prayer and of silence in us—are going to go under. Who will free us from this conflict? Who will free us from the ever-present crucifying of our real self by our ego-dominated conscious self? The answer is, always has been, that we cannot save ourself from ourself.

3. Inner → Outer

We are now going to have a look at how the inner conflict in ourselves affects the outer conflict in society and around us. I am not going to dwell on this for very long because anybody who is either in family life or in community life knows well that when they are 'out of sorts' it spreads. The inner conflict, insofar as it is unnamed, unfaced up to, unresolved, in each of us, cannot but spread to other people. My constant desire to prove myself right or to be proved right or to look good means that I have to set up people whom I can keep in their place in order that I may emerge. Very deep things that go on in any sort of community life, this inner jostling for position, and of course this desire in myself, set up conflicts and enemies and are perhaps the origin of all enmity.

The inner affects the outer in two ways. It happens through what psychatrists call *projection,* and also through what I will call *infection* (I don't know what they call it). Projection is, as you know, when I want to avoid having to face up to the conflict in myself, I find the cause for what is out of sorts in me in somebody else. I find a scapegoat. Families locate their problems onto a particular scapegoat, communities do the same. 'If we can only get rid of these dissidents then everything is going to be alright'. It is not going to be alright, but you create a public enemy to clarify the issue. We have seen this happen in a tragic way in Germany, Hitler, the Jews. We have seen almost the opposite be preached by Ghandi in India. When Indians were beginning to be persuaded that the British were the great problem they had to face, Ghandi's message, and this is always the message of non-violence and love, was that the British may be part of our problem but we are our own first enemy. Don't set up the British as the cause of what you are refusing to face within yourself.

Would that the same wisdom could emerge in Northern Ireland at the moment, where all sorts of different groups are finding simplified enemies in which to locate an external conflict instead of facing up to the unresolved conflicts in themselves. The transfer of problems from being social justice problems to do with housing and work and basic human issues, onto the presence of the British, or the army, or the unionists, or the IRA—this transference or projection, leaves each group moralistic and innocent in its own eyes.

We see the same thing happening in politics in this country. Instead of the metanoia and the conversion of ourselves we have nice clear cut enemies to blame for everything. Projection is also viciously being used in national security states, fascist states, in Latin

America and the Philippines and elsewhere. As long as you have a few 'dissidents' and 'subversives' then you have a locatable cause on which to blame all your problems so that you can avoid ever looking at the problem within. This is projection.

But there is also *infection.* That is, like it or not, know it or not, my failing to realise that the enmity and the violence within myself cannot but affect other people. We are not isolated individuals; we are part of one another. And not simply in the sense that if I am upset in the morning then my community is going to get upset too. But the actual structural conflicts in our society are contributed to by our own unresolved conflicts in ourselves. For instance, an absolute unquestioned attachment to property, which is so characteristic of our society, is also one of the effects of unresolved conflict within ourself. I know that nowadays attachment to property comes over as totally innocent, but in the preaching of Jesus and the best bits of the Church's history it has not been seen as innocent.

My attachment to things results from my failure to locate, and then to be at home in, my transcendent self. I am dominated by things insofar as I am living only with my empirical self; it is part of the domination of my ego. If I fail to resolve that, then my concern for things and property cannot but become part of the structural violence of the economics of our day. We will come back to that eventually.

4. Outer → Inner

We now have a little bit on the outer affecting the inner. This is going to be quite tricky, and I want to take it fairly quickly but fairly carefully.

The external, public violence of our day, perhaps of any day but of our day in particular, has three different temperatures. It can be hot, it can be cold and it can be cool (a little bit like something in the book of Revelation, isn't it, and remember which one had to be spat out). *Hot* violence is that of the gun or the bomb and it is certainly on the increase in the world today. I don't mean primarily that of terrorists or, which is the same from the other end, freedom fighters. What I mean is that our whole preparation for hot violence goes on innocently and deliberately all the time. In the last fifteen years the arms trade, international arms trade, has increased five fold; we are building the world up as a great arsenal, waiting for somebody to trigger something off. The armed forces in the world in the same space of time have increased by 30% until 26 million people, half the population in the United Kingdom, are now under arms, on a war footing, waiting for this or that to happen—and after all it is morally as serious to carry a hand grenade in your handbag or your pocket as it is to throw it. This is the situation we have got ourselves into.

Cold violence is the deliberate use of economic power to dominate or to destroy those who lack it. It is used in many instances by multi-national companies, for instance, in some of their operations in the poorer countries—whether it is a Japanese fishing fleet moving in on Philippino fishing boats and destroying their entire livelihood, or whether it is the Goodyear tyre company and other international companies starting beef ranches in the Amazon basin, encouraged by the Brazilian Government, at the expense and destruction of people who have been living there for centuries, who are driven off their land. This is cold violence. It might include some of the operations of supermarkets in the local high street. We could certainly include under it the machinations of unionists' industrial and political interests for fifty years in Northern Ireland. A cold violence which makes the present hot violence look like a child's game with pop guns (but of course the news media cannot locate cold violence in the same way that it can locate hot violence and somehow the British mind is trained not to recognise it too).

But I think the violence we have really got to understand is what I have called *cool* violence. It is this cool violence that gives apparent legitimation both to the hot and to the cold; so in many ways it is more basic and more important to understand.

Cool violence is that subtle and all pervasive aggression built into the fabric of a society or of a world which is concerned merely with economic prosperity and security. It is *cool* because its language is plausible and polite—'free enterprise', 'getting on in the world', 'doing your own thing', 'competition, the spice of life'—all these phrases which we take as quite normative until we happen to be reading a bit of the gospel at the same time. It is *cool* because it is plausible and polite, and it is *violence* because on the one hand it maintains two-thirds of our world in subservience and hunger, while on the other hand it deadens those who benefit from it. It is this death that I want to look at now.

What is the effect on us, our inner selves, of the economic cool violence that is endemic in our society?

Well now, are you all sitting comfortably and listening? The language and the categories with which one is able to interpret oneself and one's own experience is provided for one by the society in which one lives, by the milieu in which one is living. For most of us in this room today, we are blessed with an education and an ability to read and absorb language from many sources other than the standard one of our society. (It makes me think about the importance of spiritual reading in monastic and other life, this. Any new consciousness requires new language. If we are not to be conditioned by the limitations and one-dimensional language of contemporary daily life, it seems urgent that we keep alive much broader, much wiser, languages of interpretation. The monastic tradition has always closely linked maturity in prayer and consciousness with the art of reading wisely and reflectively—especially the Word of God in scripture. There is always the danger of forming God into an image of ourselves, of our language, rather than us being formed into his.) But for most of our contemporaries the only standard language today is economic language. It is the standard language of politicians, of the news media, of advertising. Unremittingly economic. It presents the totality of life as concerned with economic competition and material prosperity. And it presents work as an economic commodity to be bought and sold. It presents life as distinguished by what we have, not by what we are.

Now such language cannot of its very nature speak to the heart of man. However fascinating it may be, however plausible it may be, however much it may absorb us, it is essentially superficial, alienating and in the end boring (if a thing can be fascinating and boring at the same time, I believe it can). It holds out to us trivial and inaccessible goals. This language in which most of our contemporaries have to pose the central questions of identity—who am I, what is happening to me and in me, who loves me, who wants me—this standard language, which is aggressive and covetous, cannot relate to those basic fundamental questions of self-knowledge. It cannot provide an interpretation of the fundamental conflict within each of us. It cannot help anyone to know one's true self, one's true grandeur. And it cleverly legitimises the aggressive demands of the ego.

One result of this, for instance, is the general baptising, in all walks of life, of demanding-one's-own-rights. That endless game in which everyone stands up and says 'I have a duty to defend and demand my own rights—or at least the rights of "my own" '—a game which one hears very little criticised in any church quarter. We moralise about private selfishness, but are silent about its group or class equivalents. But the game has become so widespread, I believe, because of the constant economic language that people are fed and are formed by.

In such an impoverished economic language we come to interpret ourselves not as God-and-devil, but as zombies, not as saints-sinners, not as capable of anything and mean as anything, but as dull, uninteresting, open to self-hated sort of people. We are not black and white, we actually experience ourselves as grey. Erich Fromm puts it thus: 'A man sits in front of a bad television programme and does not know he is bored. He reads of casualties in the newspaper and does not recall the teachings of religion. He learns the dangers of nuclear holocaust and does not feel fear. He joins the rat race of commerce where personal worth is measured in terms of market values and is not aware of his own anxiety'. The same thing is put in a rather more exciting, perhaps excitable, way by Dorothy Sayers some time ago: 'Sloth:—in the world it calls itself Tolerance but in hell it is called Despair; it is the sin which believes nothing, interferes with nothing, enjoys nothing, loves nothing, hates nothing, finds purpose in nothing, lives for nothing and only remains alive because there is nothing it would die for'. And this terrible boredom at the basis of life today, I believe, comes because the language that our contemporaries have available for interpreting their grandeur and their meanness, their true self and their ego and so on, is simply not capable of doing so and they come to believe themselves as being grey nothings. No wonder that our confessionals are empty and our celebration is also sort of empty.

Now what happens of course is that we don't get rid of the conflict by not being able to name it or understand it; what happens is that we repress it. And there is no more dangerous state for a person to be in than to be unable to name and to face the fundamental and basic drives within. I believe this is the situation we are in. It renders one—this inability to locate and to understand and to face inner conflict (and it is one of the great achievements of polite bourgeois society, to repress this thing)—it makes one morally insensitive. As Fromm says, we cannot even recognise moral issues (which Solzhenitsyn, remember, commented on when arriving in the West). We lose the ability to suffer and that is a terrible thing for society to lose. And we learn the art of self-pity, which is almost as bad.

I would like to read to you a passage which you will know, but I read to you because it is worth hearing again—T.S. Eliot from 'The Rock':

It is hard for those who live near a Bank
To doubt the security of their money.
It his hard for those who live near a Police Station
To believe in the triumph of violence.
Do you think that the Faith has conquered the World
And that lions no longer need keepers?
Do you need to be told that whatever has been, can still be?
Do you need to be told that even such modest attainments
As you can boast in the way of polite society
Will hardly survive the Faith to which they owe their significance?
Men! polish your teeth on rising and retiring;
Women! polish your fingernails:
You polish the tooth of the dog and the talon of the cat.
Why should men love the Church? Why should they love her laws?
She tells them of Life and Death, and of all that they would forget.
She is tender where they would be hard, and hard where they like to be soft.
She tells them of Evil and Sin, and other unpleasant facts.
They constantly try to escape
From the darkness outside and within
By dreaming of systems so perfect that no one will need to be good.
But the man that is will shadow
The man that pretends to be.
And the Son of Man was not crucified once for all,
The blood of the martyrs not shed once for all,

The lives of the Saints not given once for all:
But the Son of Man is crucified always
And there shall be Martyrs and Saints.

5. The 'Lock on'

What I have tried to get a feeling for is that the latent conflict within each of us and the public conflicts of our society are in fact locked on one to another. The conflict in each, in so far as it fails to be known and recognised, even resolved, becomes one's contribution to the wider and public conflict of society; and in our present contemporary western scene that is especially dangerous because if one cannot recognise the conflict, then it becomes an irrational contribution and that is very dangerous. (National Front pay attention.) And inversely the overt or hidden conflicts of our society tend to feed-back into the inner conflict within each of us.

Now it is sometimes assumed that Christian faith says, 'Face up to the personal metanoia and liberation in yourself and the public structural liberation and peace will follow automatically. Personal conversion first and everything else will look after itself, whereas it is assumed in the opposite direction that Marxist revolutionary theory, Marxist communism says, 'Change the structural violence and people will change in themselves'. I suggest that in fact that is a misunderstanding both of Christian faith and of revolutionary theory. Luckily what we are coping with tonight is Christian faith; so we can leave the revolutionary theory for another night.

Christian faith is not about personal salvation abstracted from social realities. It is about liberation from both the inner and the outer violence, and these are both locked on to one another and doomed, until a new consciousness, a new language, can interpret the grandeur and the meanness and the conflict within us and among us.

Without a new language, violence feeds violence, and movements of liberation can do no more than create new violent people, because they are speaking the same violent language as those they try to replace. I put that clumsily; W.B. Yeats put it better:

> Hurrah for revolution and more cannon-shot!
> A beggar upon horseback lashes a beggar on foot.
> Hurrah for revolution and cannon come again!
> The beggars have changed places but the lash goes on.

The great underlying philosophy of a non-violent understanding of life is that to resolve conflict you must bring a new language which is not simply a reshaping of the existing violent language.

And that new language is never a spectator sport or the language of armchair critics. You cannot be truly non-violent, in a creative way, if you could not first be violent, because the option for non-violence presupposes the option of truly incarnational engagement. (Too many people think of non-violence as an alternative to engagement.)

This new life-interpreting and life-giving language is the task of faith. It is the insertion into this situation of the word of God—the Resurrection of Christ inserted into the situation, both of personal conflict and social conflict, a new word of life. And what we have got to do today is to rediscover that in a way that actually makes sense in our situation.

'Breaking the lock', the last part, is about how we break through this hold, this stranglehold, how we open ourselves to the answer to that terrible question that is always with us: 'Who will deliver me from this conflict, this violence within myself and in my society?'

6. Breaking the hold

I'm just going to fling out a few thoughts. I think the danger for our Church in this country at the moment is that new life is bubbling up in two ways, but each is not sufficient. New life can bubble up in a subjective enthusiasm, a sort of subjective piety that absorbs people with great vigour but does not relate to the nature of our society or face the basic questions of the political realities we are in. On the other hand there is a sort of morally serious political awareness, the sort of 'J & P business', which is seeking to be very relevant in our society but is basically unrelated to grace and to the truth of God revealed in Christ. It is a sort of secular humanism under the heading of Christianity. (I am allowed to be rude because I have been so involved in that thing.) And what we are looking for is to rediscover the word of God which will seriously face both the personal self and also the realities of our society. But it must be faithful to the gospel and that means that it must be of a living God who is present to us today and isn't dead or just watching. How are we to enable this to happen?

a) The state of feeling totally impotent, of feeling that we are up against something that is too big for any of us to cope with, that there is nothing we can do, can either lead to despair (I used to think it always led to that), or that void, waiting, feeling useless period, can free us from wanting all the solutions to be according to the way we put the problem. It can free us from our expectations and expectations of what God ought to be doing. Can't it be our loss of confidence in our expectations which is precisely what is needed as we prepare for the arrival of a new language, a new life and something truly hopeful? You may say that is just make-believe but isn't it exactly what happened to the Apostles in that upper room after the crucifixion? Didn't they have to go through that disillusionment period before the language of hope in the Resurrection and Pentecost could speak new things at all? I suspect this is necessary in every new breakthrough of consciousness down through history. It must be preceded by that awful period of feeling utterly lost and unable to do anything. It is a purifying, humbling moment, when we discover that we are blind and cannot save ourselves.

In Latin America, to give a contemporary example of the same thing, there was the period when the Christian response was equated with the guerrilla and violent response, because that seemed to be the only thing. It really got nowhere because it was speaking basically the same language of violence as those against whom it was struggling, but it seemed to be the only thing.

There was then an awful period when there seemed to be nothing at all that could be done, because the old language had gone. It had become effete and useless. And of course you can't know a new language is coming until you have a new language born. New language doesn't have a pregnancy.

What has now happened during the last two, three, four years is the appearance of the totally unexpected phenomenon of basic Christian communities bubbling up 'de baio' (from below and not all-the-solutions-from-above), which are proving more subversive, more lifegiving, more difficult for any authority that doesn't like them to cope with than anything that went before. Basically they are finding their vigour in life, not from having an enemy to fight, but by simply saying 'we are not going to expect the public authorities to solve our problems; we are going to come to life ourselves': almost exactly what Jesus was doing when those scurrilous Galileans who were beyond the law and quite hopeless, discovered in themselves the potential for life. This generates new language, new language about faith, new language about what it is to be people, people discovering in themselves a confidence and a dignity which before they had lost. These basic communities are bubbling up all over the place, not only in Latin America, but in the Philippines and elsewhere – an extraordinary phenomenon, though obviously not always successful.

I have a suspicion that in our Western Society the same sort of thing can and is beginning to happen. We are discovering, possibly afresh, what the various phrases in the Beatitudes really meant, not the terribly domesticated version that those words have come to mean in English, but what we really mean when we say 'the meek shall inherit the earth': extraordinary sense in which the real future belongs to those who know that man is too good to be violent – extraordinary, absurd, mystery.

b) We do not evolve new language, new understanding, new consciousness, simply by sitting back talking about it. It is evolved by actual concrete engagement. Scripture again and again tells us that we do not come to know God through direct knowledge. We come to know God by first of all obeying his word. This odd mystery of human knowledge and understanding and behaviour. It is only when you start to obey that you discover who it is who has given the command. It is very important in the understanding of the gospels. 'Do the will of my Father in Heaven', do not just intellectualise it. And in our case the emergence of new life, of new language and things, must involve engagement in practical action, what in Marxist theory would be called 'praxis'. And that engagement in praxis is always going to be ambiguous, is always going to be faintly absurd, is going to be laughed at by people who are so serious – they think we are going bonkers and they will tell us we are going bonkers too. But to engage in concrete and perhaps political options is very important to the emergence of new things. A Christianity which is about keeping our consciences pure, and not getting our hands dirty, is not going to generate life or hope. And getting your hands dirty is always going to question slightly whether your conscience is still pure or not. It doesn't matter too much whether or not it is pure. It is much more important that we are engaging in God's work.

c) It is, too, important that we engage the actual reality of our actual society. I say this with some feeling because when the Bishops met at Puebla, in the Latin American scene, their first question before they came up with any answers or any solutions, their first question they faced (and it is the first chapter in their document) was 'What is the reality of the society in which we are trying to live the good news? What is the reality of our Latin American society?'

Now in our case, which I suppose is vaguely paralleled by the National Pastoral Congress, that is the one question that has not been asked; so what we finish up with is a whole collection, lists, of social problems that we are going to try and solve, which are really all symptoms of the thing that we are not going to try to face. What is it about contemporary western society that makes it almost impossible for people to hear the good news as good or news? Some of us wander round as though we know the good news, and our great problem is getting it over. But I don't really think we know what the good news can mean in our inner city, in Liverpool say. People can't hear it and I think we cannot communicate it. And that is, I think, where we have got to start our questioning.

I leave you with a delightful thought that came to me as I went to sleep last night: 'Humility means that we must accept both personally and in our immediate community or family, that we are always our own first enemy. But Jesus says "love your enemy" '.

CHAPTER THREE

Of Prayer and Praxis

A few years ago, three of us were given permission to embark on a small scale monastic venture, without any explicit pastoral functions. How should the venture be described? We tried 'A House of Prayer and Hospitality'. But apart from such a description being pretentious, we abandoned it on two grounds. The hospitality proper to monastries is that of a family rather than a retreat or boarding house. Guests come to share in a life going on anyhow, not just for them. Put crudely: guests need monks not to need them.

But a more serious criticism was that monastic life is not about prayer in isolation, it is about the whole of life; it is, at least in the ideal, an interpretation of all aspects of work, eating, sleeping, study, celebrating, relating, persevering . . . and if prayer forms the integrating principle which unifies and offers the whole to God, if it is the high point of faith and of love, it is certainly not the only thing that matters, nor can it flourish if treated as an isolated world of its own.

Perhaps the strongest message that comes over in the prophets' and Jesus' teachings on prayer is their warning to religious people not to treat prayer as self-authenticating.

I find therefore that I wince at an invitation to write about 'monastic prayer'. But I warm if asked for some thoughts on the need for withdrawal as an element in everyone's life, and as epitomised in the monastic tradition.

When Moses grew up into a political awareness of the plight of his people, and got more involved than he intended by killing one of the oppressors, he withdrew from the scene. Initially this was to escape the pressures (we know the feeling? flying like a bird to one's mountain). But it turned into a mystical and very demanding encounter with God. God as unknown in himself by any head knowledge, any 'naming' knowledge, and yet truly experienced in himself in the love of the heart and its obedience to his will. I am the God who was with your people (anamnesis); you will know me in obedience to my will. I will be there.

Moses returned to the scene with a clarity and a vision of what is possible, which he could never have had as long as he remained in the scene itself.

Throughout his life we find him constantly in the dialectic of engagement—withdrawal—re-engagement. And likewise in the lives of many great figures of history: Elijah (go to the cave, what are you doing here, go back to the people). Jesus himself, involvement, withdrawal, re-involvement. And so many others.

It is a paradigm pattern for each of our lives. We start to become aware, confused, pressured in the market place; but as long as we remain there, all must be compromise, domination by the 'powers', and a fatalistic sense that life cannot be other. Withdrawal and a naked stripping before God reveal things as they are, show up the terrible mystifications of contemporary language, lay bare our own and contemporary illusions, self pities, compromises, and send us back to the market place.

It is important not to confuse this dialectic of withdrawal and engagement with any form of dualism.

The alternative to a dialectic understanding of the interdependence of prayer and the rest of life is a dualistic understanding, some sort of division of life-as-a-whole into areas where God is to be found and other areas where he is not to be found. St. Benedict, like many other monastic founders, was happily free of such dualism. If monastic life is seen as a particular way of living the gospel, the good news of a totally incarnated 'materialist' God, then there can be no areas of life which are merely neutral, no areas where we can say, with the psalmist, 'surely God does not see'.

For Benedict the daily decisions such as pricing one's produce, daily practices about shared and private ownership, about frugality or indulgence in food and drink, all these either give glory to God or do not. Such a holistic approach to life calls for great watchfulness on the part of the monk and on the part of the abbot and community in shaping the daily life of the community. It also, today, makes new demands on communities as to their economic base. At a time when our contemporaries have a heightened awareness of many social and political questions, facing radical questions about the use and misuse of natural resources, about the possession and dis-possession of means of production, about the dehumanising effects of the subtle and oppressive pressures to buy and consume more and more, at such a time a holistic and dialectic understanding of life-and-prayer will unmask, bit by bit, many inherited illusions about what gives glory to God and what does not.

It may be more important to understand, in the *Magnificat,* what is meant by 'the hungry shall have their fill and the rich be sent empty away'—as characteristic of God's dealing among men—than to search out yet another psalm tone in which to sing it. Praising and glorifying God are never self authenticating. They take their significance and value from the fundamental orientations of life as a whole.

A dualistic understanding on the other hand rests on a non-incarnational opposition between our life of prayer, solitude, contemplation, and 'the world', and is content to ignore, as not our concern, all political and economic questions, and many near-to-home daily issues of work and involvement.

It is sometimes argued that the space, freedom, and tranquility needed for a life of contemplation and intimacy with God can only be maintained if one has economic security and is free of wordly concerns. And this becomes a justification for living securely on massive endowments and investments.

Of course, all our lives are more or less ambiguous, full of unbaptised areas. But at least we can move away from bad theories and lay ourselves open, bit by bit, to what the Spirit may be trying to say to us all in these days. And that will always involve a dialectic of reflection and action, withdrawal and engagement, if we are to be released from very deep, and often dearly held, inherited illusions. No area of life remains forbidden territory.

When the true seeker (jnani) has to live in the world, his practical activity will be no less intelligent or vigorous than that of his fellows. Whatever he does will be carried out with full awareness and application. His work in the created world will at the same time be as committed and as free as that of God. He will give himself entirely to his work and yet remain totally free with regard to what he does.

God, the Absolute, manifests himself in everything; everything therefore should be done with the perfection which God's work merits. If, for example, a nun does not aim at the same perfection in her domestic duties as she does reciting the office in choir, then she is still a victim of the illusion of dualism-of-opposites (dvandva)—she has virtually decided that in her life God is more present at certain times and in certain occupations and less in others.

The teaching or nursing sister who waits impatiently for the bell to ring so that once again she can be 'with God' in chapel has not yet understood her vocation.

God is wholly present in the children she has to teach or in the sick to whom she has to minister—as Jesus taught in the clearest terms. Far from inhibiting activity, the sense of the universal presence of God is actually the greatest incentive to good work. For the true seeker there is no task which is not holy, not done in God. He does not distinguish between 'sacred' and 'profane' for him anything is holy and belongs to the Spirit's domain. He does not distinguish between the 'natural' and 'supernatural'; everything has been consecrated, taken into the divine, through Christ's incarnation. Everything, even sin and death, has been transformed by his redeeming work on the cross; everything made new by his resurrection, however little this may yet be apparent to the eye of flesh or to the mind unillumined by faith . . .

On the other hand, for all his commitment to what he is doing, he still remains supremely detached and free. For God, the Absolute, is indeed present in all his glory everywhere and in everything; yet not one of all the things in which he manifests himself is God, not one is absolute, not one has value in its own particular form [Abishiktananda, *Saccidananda,* London 1974, pp. 153f]. If monastic life, then, is holistic and dialectical we must not slide into the error of treating God as one being among other beings, prayer as one activity, one duty, among others. It is very commonplace for God and prayer to be so treated, whether by eminent theologians or organising clerics or busy monks or anyone. It is, I believe, the danger of summing up Christian life as a duty to love God and to love neighbour; the mystery of God, revealed in Christ, is not served by treating God, primarily, as an object for our love—at least not as that is commonly understood today.

Although the formal structure of daily monastic prayer is carefully and subtly integrated with the pattern of daily work, sleep, study, meals etc., St Benedict nevertheless invites us to allow nothing to come before the *Opus Dei,* the work of God. And this central, and ever so difficult, principle—difficult because time wasted with God is always threatened by any other activities which have feed back for our ego—this central principle comes not from some magical approach to prayer as being self-authenticating (sort of *opus operandum*) nor from some idea that God needs our prayer and praise.

The primacy of prayer, and therefore the importance of withdrawal in the life of any person of faith, not just the monk, comes from the very nature of God himself and the fact that everything else in life, one's own self and all one's relationships, are at root nothing but participations in the being and the life of God. As long as we experience ourselves as autonomous and our relationships as standing in their own right, we have not yet grasped God—or been grasped by God—as he who is our only true being. We are away from home, alienated, scattered and at odds both within and among ourselves as long as we have not found ourselves in God.

This is very difficult for the modern mind to accept because Western history for the last few centuries has brought us to a concept of our 'self' as autonomous. To be a full person is to be an isolated self, an independent being, 'true to itself', doing its own thing. And to a mind thus conditioned God will always seem as something 'other', prayer as a forced and rather unnatural obligation, obedience as de-humanising, asceticism as more or less masochistic, and a loss of self concern as a loss of everything!

What in fact awakens in the heart of anyone who perseveres in prayer, who is willing to create the necessary space and to say 'no' to many other (quite legitimate) things which crowd in on life today, who is willing to journey through the abandonments and pain which prayer must involve at certain times, what awakens is an acute sense of being at home in God—and nowhere else. In the scriptural and Catholic traditions, certainly in the writings of the best mystics in our tradition, holiness and union with God is, as it were, more natural to man than all else in life. But it always involves an abandonment of every other attachment—even an abandonment of our affection for, attachment to, God's most beautiful creatures. What is not rendered up can never be received back as gift, what is not lost as conscious attachment cannot be received back 'in God'. The bread and wine have to be handed over if they are to be received back as 'communion'. Possessing nothing, all the world is one's own—in God.

Withdrawal is not therefore merely spatial or temporal, not merely finding a place or a time to get away. It involves a genuine poverty of spirit, and a constant repeated turning of the mind away from all involvements, all aggressions and resentments, all regrets and desires, a turning away from all experienced at the surface until the heart becomes accustomed to being at home at its centre point. For there is at the very centre of our being, at the still point, at the true self, that which simply is God. The chaotic instruments which make up our orchestra bit by bit come into a concerted whole under the loving and persistent guidance of our composer-cum-conductor. We come to a strange and quite unexpected peace, a peace which makes the bourgeois security-based peace of earlier times look like a sick joke, but a peace which brings with it an opening out into communion not a closing in on self.

The great surprise, at least to the modern mind, is that the most central reality of life is not after all an isolated and autonomous self, but communion.

Most of us grow into God not as snails or centipedes, but as grasshoppers. Something happens to us, perhaps quite suddenly or over some time, and we look back and realise we are not what or where we were. The view has changed too.

Breakthroughs of awareness, expansions of the heart, are normally recognisable only by hindsight. The Lord was there and I knew it not. But we can make *anamnesis,* learn from our experience, what to expect. Such quanta jumps always involve some leap into the unknown, and therefore call us to abandon what is familiar. They are usually in response to some specific demand made on us, either clearly (as in the case of the rich young man in the gospel) or in the more obscure understanding of our own situation, or of social realities. (Many in the Church have, in recent years, discovered an intimacy with God by becoming aware of social and political realities.) Nearly always there is some blockage which holds us back from breaking through—or being broken through. It may be some self indulgence, some intellectual fixation, some clinging to our ego or good name, some 'indispensable' vested interest or security (as for the rich young man who simply 'could not' go, sell, give, come, follow).

These successive breakthroughs are true not only for individuals, but also for communities, and indeed for local Churches. Some jump, some don't.

But there are two breakthroughs in particular which I would like to mention.

When we set out, enthusiastically, to follow the Lord, to seek God, things seem more or less controllable. We know what we are about, we feel we know God, and life is lived more or less at a moral level. God is pretty lucky to have us around to do his will.

Suffering, patient endurance, lack of achievement even (especially?) in the things of God, aridity in prayer, all set in sooner or later. Our inflated self image is deflated, we wonder what happened to our ideals and clarity. But perseverance brings us through to a new freedom. No longer 'I come to do your will' but 'May your will be done in me'. No longer the question 'What can I do for my Lord', but 'What will the Lord do in me?' Prayer is experienced no longer as that which I do for, to, or at God, but rather as the space in which God enters. Prayer happens to us, and *Opus Dei* comes to mean the work of God among us, God's work in us rather than our work for God. We come to be far less concerned about our moral rightness, and far more about responding to what God is working in and around us – an incarnational response which happily risks getting hands dirty, taking risks, standing up to be counted, and is not too concerned about the state of one's own soul.

This transition is beautifully described by Carol Bieleck, R.S.C.J.:

> I built my house by the sea.
> Not on the sands, mind you;
> not on the shifting sand.
> And I built it of rock.
> A strong house
> by a strong sea.
> And we got well acquainted, the sea and I.
> Good neighbours.
> Not that we spoke much.
> We met in silences.
> Respectful, keeping our distance,
> but looking our thoughts across the fence of sand.
> Always, the fence of sand our barrier,
> always, the sand between.
>
> And then one day,
> – and I still don't know how it happened –
> the sea came.
> Without warning.

Without welcome, even
Not sudden and swift, but a shifting across the sand
like wine,
less like the flow of water than the flow of blood.
Slow, but coming.
Slow, but flowing like an open wound.
And I thought of flight and I thought of drowning
and I thought of death.
And while I thought the sea crept higher, till it
reached my door.
And I knew, then, there was neither flight, not death,
nor drowning.
That when the sea comes calling you stop being
good neighbours
Well acquainted, friendly-at-a-distance, neighbours
And you give your house for a coral castle,
And you learn to breath underwater.

The other breakthrough I would like to mention is this: if a life of prayer, and the necessary withdrawal it implies, matures in a wholesome way, it cannot but lead to a real agony of awareness as regards evil in the world and the terrible affliction of so many of one's brothers and sisters—weighed down by hunger or disease, dispossessed of any cultural participation ... Indeed prayer should and often does make a person not only aware of these things but far more sensitive and vulnerable to them. A great sense of impotence sets in, a great longing to be effective. That hunger may be a call to go and engage at the front line, to live among the afflicted, but most often it is a more demanding call to live for (and with) them in whatever position one is in.

As one awakens to God as the heart of all one's

reality, one awakens also to a deeper self knowledge; but also one awakens to a cosmic communion with all people. This is not the coming of any new relationship, but the discovering of that fundamental communion which preexists our awareness of it. But our awareness of it cannot but open up quite new demands on our response—unless we are to spiritualise that awareness and refuse the dialectic between prayer and praxis. Our communion with people, especially the afflicted, calls us to a practical love with political, economic, and life-style implications. We can no longer be content with love as the art of getting on with our own brothers or sisters in community, or family, or work or wherever. (Even the pagans know that art, do they not.) Nor can we argue that such expansions of love do not concern those called to other things.

Years ago our novice master said: learn to exclude no one from your love. But at that time we could not yet know what demands of honesty, suffering, and exhilaration that would involve as God awakens the heart to himself, to one's self, and to all people.

> Not one of our fellowmen, even if he wished, could fail us. In the most unfeeling miser, in the innermost being of the prostitute, in the foulest drunkard, there is an immortal soul intent on keeping alive, but which, being shut out from the light of day, worships in the night. I hear them speaking when we speak, and weeping when I kneel to pray. I accept all this! I reach out to them all. There is not one that I do not need, not one that I can do without! There are many stars in the sky and their number is beyond me, yet there is not one I do not need in order to praise God. There are many people

alive on earth and we see hardly more than a few who stand out and shine while the others wander as in a world of chaos. Yes there are many souls, but there is not a single one with whom I am not in communion through that sacred spot in it that says, 'Our Father' [Paul Claudel, *Black Pearl*].

CHAPTER FOUR

The Psalms and The Poor

Foreword

It is probably commonplace among psychiatrists, but I have been too slow as a priest to appreciate that it is not helpful to tell a person in distress that he should not be feeling the way he does. 'Cheer up!' is seldom constructive. True compassion sits beside a person; it does not stand in front, push from behind or say 'Come over here', unless to help him gently to take himself less seriously or see things from a wider viewpoint. Always it knows that a person has within himself inner resources, however slight, which are the only strengths that can really provide any long-term way through. Ready advice or clever truisms do more to feed the priest's or counsellor's self-esteem that provide healing or joy to the one who suffers.

No person should expect or be expected to live always at Pentecost, and it does not help on Good Friday for one to be told one should be at Pentecost (or Easter, for that matter).

The Psalms never tell us that we should not be

feeling the way we are. They start prayer where we are—depressed, angry, envious, elated, awestruck; they take the full range of our ambiguous human experience seriously. There is no mood from which prayer cannot start. They journey with us on our way, working depression and self-pity through to wonder, unholy anger through to holy anger, feelings of God's absence through to confidence in his presence. They journey with us and never tell us we should not be where we are.

This is one reason, I believe, why the psalms have had such amazing staying-power as Jewish and Christian prayer.

Before considering some particular psalms, there are two other thoughts I would like to share.

Many of us have been educated out of speaking, let alone writing, 'gut language'. We find it impossible to state what our real feeling-responses are to life, how our hearts really react to things. All is stated with care, and then qualified, and then footnoted.

But many of the psalms are gut-language, especially the cursing psalms (politely omitted from the Roman Office) and those calling on God's anger. If we could get down on paper what we really feel when we hear of a violent attack on an innocent family in Belfast, or a really dishonest business deal, or the blatant and oppressive injustice of modern police states, would our hearts not write similar prayers? But we don't write like that. And if we did we would immediately correct it in the second draft with other expected niceties about loving our enemies, and praying for persecutors. Not that these are wrong; indeed they are our true self responding to our initial reaction. My point is that some of the psalms are *first reaction* prayer, where we still know the importance of God's anger, and not only of his mercy. I once read a passage from the first chapters of Romans to some boys, without giving its source. One of them remarked: 'Thank goodness the Christian New Testament has done away with that horrible vindictive God of the Old'. But it seems to me that Jesus and his followers took up rather than rejected the Jewish interpretation of history and the anger-and-mercy of God. It is selective amnesia to ignore the hard warnings of Jesus (especially towards the end) and many hard passages in the Epistles and Revelation.

I was recently talking to a priest about our inability to appreciate the anger of God and how the moral lassitude of our modern society was just the occasion which scripture warns us about—everyone fast asleep in bed—when history turns over and God's presence is revealed in suffering and anger, not in well-being and blessings. He thought all that was nonsense, that scriptural language of struggle and anger belonged to primitive ages and that the great step of being civilized was to grow out of all that into a universal caring and peacefulness.

Many of the psalms are spoken by a man struck low, or voice a *cri de coeur* for the oppressed over against the powerful and established. It is indeed as unthinkable that the psalms could be written within the walls of a comfortable presbytery, monastery or convent, as it is unthinkable that protest songs could be written by the polite guitar-playing groups which so often sing them.

This, I believe, poses a real question to those of us who pray the psalms and yet by no stretch of the imagination can pretend to belong to the *malheur innocent,* the innocent afflicted of the world. As Vincent McNabb said years ago, in a letter to Walter Shewring, it is strange indeed 'that we can read them daily for a lifetime without realizing that after the essential and primary topic of the soul's relation to God, the next topic seems to be the poor'. It has become even stranger since having the psalms in English.

The word often used for the poor in the psalms is *ana,* meaning *bent down*—under pressures of social injustice, illness, destitution. Such people belonged in a special way to God because they belonged to no-one else. Their poverty was not the holy simplicity which some of us romanticize about today, but the unholy poverty which destroys people and which is utterly rejected by the psalmists and prophets. God will vindicate them and the established well-to-do religious people ignore them at their peril.

It was only a further development which gave *ana* the spiritual connotation of being bent down, humble, before God, so that the *anawim* became those capable of appreciating God because of their basic simplicity. This was a holy poverty in no way rejected. It is dangerous, however, to confuse these two—unholy poverty which is scandal in God's eyes, and holy poverty which is essential to his kingdom.

Perhaps we find the distinction in Luke's and Matthew's versions of the Sermon on the Mount. Luke begins, 'Blessed are you poor'—the coming of the Kingdom brings authentic hope to you; you who have previously been despised and unwanted are now at the centre of the picture. Matthew begins, 'Blessed are the poor in spirit'—you who know your need of God (though Matthew would have no illusions that one can be poor-in-spirit internally, without it affecting and being affected by the way one lives and the pursuits one pursues).

The psalms do not pray much *for* the poor; they pray rather *with* or *as* the poor. Those of us who pray them are thereby committed to something much deeper than 'a paternal charity for the poor and the sick' (Vatican II). We are called to identify rather than to serve.

It was Belfast, after nearly twenty years as a monk, which brought home many of the psalms to me. Issues of life and death, of struggle, of oppression and freedom, of violence and peace – these can be so easily domesticated by Latin plainchant. It was empathy with Latin-American Christians which revealed the *Magnificat* to me as a powerful liberation song about God's ways of turning history downside up; before that it had been only the song of a Jewish maiden.

It is not, I think, at all easy for us to appreciate the mystery of the Church's identification with the poor, with the *malheur innocent,* and her consequent non-identification with, indeed antipathy towards, any political or economic processes which do not take them seriously. I recall one psalm-pray-er arguing sincerely that 'we have no really poor in our society today', yet Mother Teresa can say that she finds a deeper poverty in our urbanized, industrialized society than anything she has known in Calcutta.

It is not easy for us to appreciate the Church's, our, identification with the poor because (a) our spirituality is still very private and individualistic; (b) our theology is over-academic and removed both from mystical theology and also from a real engagement with people-in-their-history, people in the concrete realities of their lives (in our case, the realities of today's western society); (c) we still think in terms of nation-states at a time when the reality of our existence binds us irrevocably with the destitute in any part of the world; and (d) because we can hardly appreciate our deep participation in the cosmic evil in our world.

To pray the psalms authentically cannot but affect a person's life-style, world-view, economic and political decisions . . . How can people say that the Church is not involved in politics when they pray the psalms daily?

Perhaps we shall have to re-learn from the coming Third Church what we are already in fact committed to:

> Our theology (and prayer?) is not an automatic mental and spiritual process. We are not at peace with our own theology . . . Theology is not a detached, objective, cool, neutral, analytical observation of God. We are finding out in our 'theology in action' that 'cool theology', of all variations, cannot really nourish us, no matter how imposing and historic. Does detached, objective, cool, neutral, analytical observation of man interest you? If it does, you may be interested in detached, objective, cool, neutral, analytical observation of God.

Psalm 73

Nikos Kazantzakis's strange and powerful book, *The Last Temptation,* depicts Jesus' final struggle as an acute form of the temptation which must beset anyone who has 'left all to follow': the nagging fear, that is, that the whole venture was a mistake, that he has in the end risked all for absurdity.

Within the affectionate household of Martha, Mary and Lazarus at Bethany, Jesus looks back with nostalgia to Nazareth and wonders whether he would not have served his Father better by leading a quite normal family life, remaining a carpenter, perhaps marrying Mary of Bethany, not chasing after the risky calling of a prophet, but rather baptizing normal everyday family life.

Why take on the risks and the vulnerability? Why take on a life of impotent poverty? Why force home a message which could not but divide people, could not but 'reveal the hearts of many'? Why force ultimate issues in a way that must threaten so many good people? What sort of loving Father could be served by such churlishness?

Such an interpretation of Jesus' ultimate struggle may stretch the evidence but it does surely represent a real temptation, perhaps the last temptation, of any person dedicated in a special way 'for the sake of the kingdom', whether religious, priest or lay. Psalm 73 is that person's psalm.

How good God is to those who are pure of heart.

Purity of heart is that in us which corresponds to oneness and fidelity in God. It is to be 'consequent on one's belief', to be willing, without arrogance, to refuse compromise, to be ready to abandon all to follow, to sell all for the pearl of great price. In Jesus' preaching, purity of heart is the opposite of double-mindedness, double-think, religious hypocrisy. It is the opposite of that in each of us which, finding a sense of security and purpose in professing Christ and even being clever at preaching him, yet fails to translate the gospel into practice, fails to take risks in his name, fails in fact to do the will of his Father. Perhaps 'renewal' is precisely the closing of this gap, learning the singleminded art of admitting God into the practical daily affairs of life-style, the use of money, business practices, administration, social relationships and so on.

Yet my feet came close to stumbling,
I was filled with envy of the proud
when I saw how the wicked prosper.

'Wickedness', 'pride', 'sin' have moral overtones today which they had not for the psalmist. For us today one is only wicked if one knows one is, if one has some conscious intention to do evil. Sin is individual and it is conscious. But for the psalms and scripture in general, sin is at once more social and more objective. One is wicked not because one feels wicked, but because *de facto* one is engaged in work against the law of God, against the Kingdom. If the wicked or the proud do not realise what they are doing (and in general we/they surely do not), that makes things worse not better.

The psalmist, here, sees such go-getters 'doing well for themselves', 'getting on in the world', and feels an agony of envy; all the cards seem stacked for worldly pursuits and success, while he has nothing to show for the alternative life he has chosen.

For them there are no pains,
their bodies are sound and sleek.
They have no share in men's sorrows.

All of us who happen, by birth, fortune or pursuit, to enjoy bodies that are sound and sleek, are in permanent danger of never discovering our identity with men and women at large, or, having discovered it, of opting out. As a lady said to me last week, the nature of all privilege is to want to go it alone. 'Going it alone' is a form of illusion, of unreality. It is to belong to a special and smaller world than that in which God has placed us. Today it is doubly unreal because of the close interconnectedness and interdependence of all nations and classes on one another. A meditation in our larder on the human histories involved in bringing our taken-for-granted food to our table is sufficient to remind us of this, and perhaps too to convince us that the rich depend on the poor more than the poor on the rich.

'I do not say: You are damned if you have possessions', said Augustine, commenting on this psalm. 'You are damned if you take them for granted, if you are puffed up by them, if you think yourself important because of them, if because of them you forget the poor, if you forget your common human status because you have more of what are vanities'.

So they wear their pride like a necklace.

It has been suggested that this psalm borrowed its imagery from an annual ceremony in a local pagan city during which a water god was drawn out of the river, paraded through the streets and bedecked with garlands. The people would 'turn to follow . . . drinking it all in', singing and dancing.

The psalmist transposes this pagan idolatry and allurement to the idolatry of worldly pursuits, success and wealth, seeing in them the root cause of self-satisfaction, pride and blindness.

The imagery may, however, be more direct: the psalmist sees that the prosperous, being removed from the common lot of men, become proud and violent in ways that are as much a part of them as a badge of office or the clothes they wear. 'Pride is their collar of jewels and violence the robe that wraps them' (NEB).

Either way we know, from so much today, just what the psalmist is talking about. What is not so clear, though, and we certainly fail to preach, is that a one-dimensional pursuit of God's material blessings leads to a fundamental, pervasive and unrecognised forgetfulness of God.

> Take heed, lest, when you have eaten and are full, and have goodly houses and live in them, and your silver and gold is multiplied, then your heart be lifted up and you forget the Lord your God. Beware lest you say in your heart 'My power and the might of my hand have got this wealth'. Remember the Lord your God, for it is he who gives you power . . . If you go after other gods and serve them . . . you will surely perish [Deut. 8].

And more recently, Abraham Lincoln warned:

> We have been the recipients of the choicest bounties of heaven; we have been preserved these many years in peace and prosperity; we have grown in

numbers, wealth and power as no other nation has ever grown. But we have forgotten God. We have forgotten the gracious hand which preserved us in peace and multiplied and enriched and strengthened us, and we have vainly imagined, in the deceitfulness of our hearts, that all these blessings were produced by some superior wisdom and virtue of our own. Intoxicated with unbroken success, we have become too self-sufficient to feel the necessity of redeeming and preserving grace, too proud to pray to the God that made us. It behoves us, then, to humble ourselves before the offended Power, to confess our national sins and to pray for clemency and forgiveness' [30 March, 1863].

Although we may not, as a nation, feel quite so secure today, his words express a perennial wisdom. Indeed if we view our assumed life-styles within the context of the world at large, or of history at large, we discover most of our social and psychological problems to be the inevitable results of being pampered, of taking too much for granted and of trying to 'dictate to the earth'. They are not the real sorrows related to a lack of basic needs.

They have set their mouths in the heavens
and their tongues dictate to the earth.

It seems inevitable for any human endeavour which loses a sense of being responsible to something higher than itself that its power breeds greater power, its technology breeds more centralised technology, its capital breeds capital. These tendencies perpetuate or widen the gap between those who have and those who have not, those who pull the strings and those who survive as best they can. And the ultimate outcome is militarism and/or fascism, whether in its subtle forms throughout our society, or its brutal overt forms in police states, whether of the left or the right.

This worldly tendency to turn power and ability in upon themselves, for their own ends, is absolutely set against the divine order. If political and economic pressures are to be shaped by the latter, and so participate in God's liberating will for people, certain attitudes need to be fostered until they are second nature, until they emerge in the practical decisions which shape people's lives. (For politics and economics to incarnate the Kingdom, a spirituality is required.) These basic attitudes are that people matter most, that economic development is always secondary to integral whole-person development, and that all abilities, like material benefits, are always God's gift and therefore for sharing.

Such attitudes will not dominate or centralise. They will encourage local initiative, community action (especially amongst the least likely), and the turning outwards, to serve people, of capital, technology, influence, trade.

It is remarkable how often Paul VI returned to the importance of people-participation as the essential antidote to the diverse centralism of power in modern societies. And it is this basic incarnational intuition that is forcing many hierarchies to stand with God's lowliest people over against the policies of their governments—governments who are more interested in national security and getting in on a development based on international western capitalism than they are in the life and participation of their humblest citizens.

Man plays God in order to dictate to the earth. He flies in the face of God who played man in *kenosis and for others.*

So people turn to follow them.

Ritchie Calder, years ago, described the general mood present in every corner of our modern world, from the remotest African village or Eskimo camp to our own big cities, as 'a revolution of rising expectations'. Transistor radios, the news media and easy travel have put everyone in instant contact with everyone else. Everyone knows how the other half lives, and this knowledge breeds discontent—a healthy discontent in enabling the destitute to know that, after all, life does not have to be as it is—an unhealthy discontent, in great and small alike, if they cannot be at peace in life as it is.

Modern economic process has to create needs in people, it depends and thrives on a consumer hunger in people.

TV commercials tell people, in effect, that a family has not arrived if it does not enjoy the good looks, the easy life, portrayed on the screen. But in many less obvious ways bandwagons (like water gods?) fascinate, invite and always disappoint.

I think of the effects of western tourism in poor countries, blatantly displaying untroubled affluence alongside subsistence living and generating among the dispossessed both an admiring fascination and a deep sense of inadequacy. I think of millions who have moved off their lands in search of urban life and end up in the squalid shanties surrounding most great cities today—a movement partly caused by the breakdown of rural economics and partly by the pull of urban life—but both parts caused by westernised elites and governments favouring 'development' in prestige projects and in countries that favour foreign capital rather than modest, unseen but vital development of agriculture and village life.

They say 'How can God know? Does he take any notice?'

This phrase appears in various forms in other psalms. The fool says in his heart 'There is no God'. The boastful thinks in his heart 'God forgets, he does not see'. 'There is no God; he will not punish'. The psalmist is not referring to explicit denial of God, atheism. He is referring to those areas of life which we never bring under the light of faith, because we are conditioned not to, because we are too busy, or because we have an intuitive foresight that vested interests are endangered if we do. Those many areas of Monday to Friday living remain neutral, free of any serious critique or sense of answerability.

I have recently been involved in gathering a series of passages, from the Fathers and from Encyclicals, on 'property' (C.T.S. *Mine and Thine, Ours and Theirs*). The seriousness with which they bring the Gospel to bear on practical issues of ownership and its social character is striking. It is not that I used to have one idea about what owning things means, and now I am having to revise it. It is rather that I used to have no idea at all. And that is true I would think of nearly everyone in our society. In fact our industrial, capitalist, consumer economy has grown up largely free of any serious Christian critique. Religion has been kept for church and the bedside, and the implications of ownership have been left in that large neutral amoral area where God does not see.

Yet the nature of ownership and the basic processes of production of man's material needs are the animators of all social and political activity. Marx was right in this and he is vindicated by what is happening in all parts of the world today. It is these questions which lie behind South African apartheid, Northern Ireland bitterness, South American and Philippine fascism, Cambodian genocide, the machinations of multinational companies (answerable to no-one), and indeed the struggles of management and unions here at home.

Paul VI and an increasing number of national hierarchies and theologians in the third world have focussed on such questions as by no means 'neutral'. For their efforts they are dubbed communist by other Christians with too many vested interests (and so would half the saints we celebrate on our altars, from Basil, John Chrysostom and Gregory to Thomas Aquinas). But in our western societies, Europe and America, there is a strange conspiracy of silence underwritten by pious remarks about 'the Church must keep out of politics'.

If God is God, can any area of life remain neutral? And do we not find today a greater hunger in people for an interpretation of their daily life some sort of meaning, the shedding of some sort of light, however unwelcome, on their daily pre-occupations, business, economics, work . . . ? Religion will remain one colossal yawn for our contemporaries as long as our Church involvement concerns itself primarily with our Church involvement.

Perhaps many of us are afraid of such issues because we are basically good-mannered and courteous, for little can be said without the danger of being churlish or saying the wrong thing. But the alternative is not in fact neutrality, however much we hope it is, but rather the Church's tacit support of much that the gospel and her real tradition has never accepted. *Qui tacet consentire videtur.*

The psalmist sees himself, then, in the midst of the world doing well for itself, finds himself surrounded by the prosperous, while he himself seems to have taken the fool's path, unrecognized, ineffective. He is sorely tempted. How useless to keep his heart pure, absurd, naive to pursue poverty when it gets him nowhere. Worse—he is stricken for his efforts, suffers punishment all the day. (The suffering, perhaps, which is invited by integrity and so powerfully portrayed in the early chapters of Wisdom, the lives of the prophets, and the life of Jesus.)

My feet had almost slipped. Then I said,
'if I speak like that I betray the race of your sons'.

At the brink of throwing in his lot, a profound spirituality confronts his temptation. A spirituality which involves (a) a scriptural interpretation of history, (b) a realization that all worldly pursuits outside the milieu of God turn to illusion, idolatry, dream, phantom, and (c) a simple and utter conviction that innocence and integrity of life, in the presence of God, can never be in vain—however unlikely it seems. The meek shall inherit the earth. The first two (a) and (b) we must consider elsewhere. A word about the third.

It is consoling that the psalmist 'strove to fathom this problem' and found it 'too hard for his mind to understand' until he 'pierced the mysteries of God'. It is characteristic of our own scientific and rational age to want rational answers to our problems, and thus to be suspicious of the apparent inefficiency of faith. The intuition of faith convinces me that authentic love born of innocence and integrity can never be wasted nor ineffectual, that non-violence and peace building are somehow more effective than violence, that doing right, because it is right, is more lifegiving than endless scheming and bending to pragmatic solutions, that the sermon on the Mount does make sense, and that the Cross is for real—it is not some divine magic which somehow turns tragedy into comedy. These things I find I believe, but I do not understand how or why.

There is, of course, a false innocence which hopes to engage with God by disengaging with his world, as if the Creator could despise or ignore his creation. But when the psalmist sings 'I was always in your presence ... What else have I in heaven but you? Apart from you I want nothing on earth', he is not, I think, slipping into this naive innocence. Rather he is speaking of that God-centredness which alone can free us from ambition and personal ego, from personal loss or gain, from personal interest; and it is only with liberation from these personal interests that our engagement in the world can be fully serious and true—not for our sake, but for its sake and for the glory of God. It is not escape, it is involvement. A person cannot escape the washing up merely by talking to the Guest.

Likewise there is a false integrity which is self-righteous, perhaps arrogant, even brutal. It constantly feeds its ego on the infantile conviction, 'I'm right and all of you are wrong'. In effect it believes that it possesses truth rather than being in some way possessed by it.

But the innocence and integrity of the psalmist is strong yet humble, serious yet detached, engaged yet without personal interest. We find it in much folklore (I think of Frodo in *The Lord of the Rings*) and in the lives of so many of the saints. Indeed the last verses of psalm 73 read very much like St Teresa's book-mark (A lady of great action and vigour!):

> Let nothing disturb you
> Let nothing dismay you
> All things pass;
> God never changes.
> Patience attains
> All that it strives for
> He who has God
> Finds he lacks nothing:
> God alone suffices.

Psalm 146

Sometime ago I was at a Christian Aid meeting. We were discussing the theological meaning of such work when someone said, 'Would it not be ironical if, after four hundred years of Reformation history, we all end up trying to justify ourselves by good works?' An immediate ah-ha response came from everyone present, for the remark touched a sensitive point which everyone there knew to be crucial.

At a time when Christians generally are far more socially conscious than before and many are politically active, the question of how such activity for the oppressed or marginal or forgotten really relates to God and Christ and the Kingdom needs to be asked honestly. It is quite possible for Christians to be vigorously involved with prisoners, with the homeless, with the sick, with international issues of justice, but in fact to have a God who is no more than a spectator and a Christ who is no more than a moral teacher.

It may be, of course, that they are closer to God in doing his will than those who cry, 'Lord, Lord!' but do it not. But then you don't have to be a Christian for that. The sheep in the parable, those invited into the eternal life prepared for them, were surprised because they did not know how their service of the hungry, naked, imprisoned was in effect service of Christ. Whereas the goats, who seemed to believe in Christ, were surprised because they didn't realise that in ignoring the dispossessed they were ignoring Christ. That is food for thought, of course. But our present question is how to integrate both sides, how to interpret social caring in the light of authentic faith in God.

I suspect that we are all conditioned more than we can understand by secular humanism. We may not altogether agree that the scientific and technological revolutions have issued in man's 'coming of age', nor that, as a result, God is no longer really needed—even if he is nice to have around (given that he is not actually dead). Nevertheless we cannot avoid having a sense of man's competence, nor feeling uneasy about how God fits in to our world and in what way the initiative remains his not ours. After all, man's 'coming of age' is only a new name for Pelagius's heresy, a very British heresy!

He is happy whose hope is in the Lord His God,
who alone made heaven and earth,
the seas and all they contain.

One of the reasons for our dilemma is that Christian debate and theology since the Reformation has been largely to do with Christ, sin and redemption. We have been talking about Christians, the Church and salvation but not much about humanity and creation. We have come, perhaps unwittingly, to think of God's domain of action as co-terminous with the Church, to think of the locus of God's grace in the individual Christian and in the Church, rather than in people, just as people, and the world as such. A spirituality based on such exclusiveness will not feed us now that we are a small minority in a largely secular world.

The psalms and the mystics, however, assume a far wider and more profound context. They take us to the heart of God as total and absolute creator. The One in whom all people live and move and have their being, the One whose Spirit pervades and activates the lives of all people (not merely those who acknowledge it), the One whose word and wisdom pervades all history, personal and social.

I personally find this easy to say but almost impossible to believe in any living, real, enduring way. I suppose this is because ours is not an age of faith and I am part of the age. And yet I feel intuitively that a contemplative theology of creation and of people is a necessary context today in which to understand the mystery of Christ and the Church. Until I can appreciate people, the people I meet and the people I know about, as the primary locus of God's grace; until I can somehow grasp that 'no love is ever lost', in whomever's heart and hands God gives it shape; until then I will still have an exclusive and rather arrogant idea of the Church and of Christian love. (The sort of arrogance betrayed in phrases like 'Christians and all men of good will'.)

And worse still! I may even be left with a sort of fortress mentality with clean cut distinctions between insiders and outsiders, between those who are loyal and those who are subversive, between good people and bad people. Such social Manichaeism is rampant today.

Of course, of course, many of the psalms are Manichaean in the same way. God is a god of the virtuous and the psalmist is convinced that his enemies must be God's enemies also. But somehow one can pray through that, applying a bit of mental reservation, or allowing for cultural distance, or for the development of ethical norms. The main point is that the psalmist's God is a God of creation, of people, of history, of love and of anger. A total God not a partial God. A God who can only be known and praised in a clashing of Symbols, and is not to be confined by anyone's understanding, not even the Church's.

> How good is the Lord to all,
> compassionate to all his creatures . . .
> Your friends . . . shall speak of the glory of your reign
> and declare your might, O God,
> to make known your mighty deeds
> and the glorious splendour of your reign (Psalm 145).

Given that God is God of all, that he is utterly faithful (he will achieve his purposes . . .) and also merciful (. . . in spite of our stupidity), then the Church exists precisely to bear witness to and celebrate God's universal presence and work. It is for the Christians to make explicit in their life what is normally implicit in most people, to acknowledge what is normally anonymous, to reveal what is otherwise hidden: the universal and redeeming love of God. It is for Christians, the Church, to generate a language, a consciousness, *a praxis,* which expresses that which is latent in all people and the whole of history. Especially a *praxis,* for witness 'does not lie in engaging in propaganda nor even in stirring people up, but in being a living mystery. It means to live in such a way that one's life would not make sense if God did not exist' (Cardinal Suhard).

In precise terms: the Church is not the Kingdom, but she is a sign of the Kingdom.

Furthermore, since human behaviour and history are intimately bound up with human consciousness—how we see and talk generates how we behave and what we become—then the Church by revealing in her life and her language the hidden mysteries of God becomes an effective instrument of God in achieving his purpose. In short she (that is we) is not merely a sign, but an effective sign, a sacrament of the Kingdom.

I find this approach is far from abstract ecclesiology. For one thing it introduces a whole-life spirituality in place of a private soul-saving one. The key question becomes of what significance, what sign-value, does our life have? Is it an icon of God or is it conformed to one of the many substitute kingdoms of human's devising?

And it also helps to answer our original dilemma. That is, it provides an interpretation of the relationship between Christian Aid and Oxfam, say; between Catholic Housing Aid and other work for the homeless;

between a Prison Chaplain and others who serve prisoners; between religious sisters in a hospital and the other sisters and nurses. Indeed it interprets the role of any identifiable Christian body in secular fields of education, politics, community action . . . Each is saying in some way:

> *It is God who is just to the oppressed,*
> *It is he who gives bread to the hungry,*
> *the Lord who sets prisoners free,*
> *who gives sight to the blind,*
> *who raises up those who are bowed down,*
> *who protects the stranger,*
> *and upholds the widow and orphan.*

These are challenging lines and I am not sure I know what they mean. But:

a) They do not mean that God works in *spite* of us, by some magic. The whole scriptural stance is that God has elected to work within history, and through our responsibility. The Adam myth is a firm statement of this.
b) God never has to be won over on to our side, in the way some bidding prayers and graces imply when they pray for the hungry. Jesus was very clear in the Sermon on the Mount. Our heavenly Father is far more concerned for the forgotten than we can ever be. The problem is winning us over on to his side. He is the faithful one; *it is God who keeps faith forever.*
c) I think these lines are a marvellous affirmation of what I tried to say earlier: that all authentic love

is incorporation into the will and work of God, even if for most people it is never recognized as such. No love is lost (if authentic) precisely because it springs from the heart of God.

d) I think they say also that if you seek God, you must allow his likeness to grow in you, and this can happen only if you behave like him. (This is the original idea of the Jewish Torah.) If God loves all people he necessarily shows a bias to the otherwise unloved. Hence he turns human structures, politics and history upside down—for these are ever favouring the favoured. To be like God is effectively to engage in the same work.

e) Finally, these lines have a suspicion of the inevitable about them. God will achieve his purpose; he will feed and free and protect and uphold. To join in this is to join in what is real. To opt out is to abandon what is real (however promising the current alternatives may appear). The dance goes on, we are invited to join in (we can learn the steps as we shuffle around), but remaining a wallflower is far more secure. The dance, however, goes on—with or without us. God's word does not return to him ineffective.

Some people argue, at least by implication, that unless a person is actively involved in serving the poor or working for the oppressed, one cannot be following Christ. That is a very one-dimensional limitation of the catholicity of God and of the poor themselves, let alone the vast majority of people who are called to the daily routines of ordinary life.

There is however something normative in the above

lines of the psalm (echoed by the prophets and claimed as his own by Jesus in the synagogue at Nazareth, Luke 4:18–22). They provide a basic thought pattern, a basic world-view, which is integral to Christian faith and provides an ever present assessment of whatever else we are involved in. It will liberate us from the dangers of small-worldly and bourgeois self preoccupation.

To say that God is alive in the lives of all people and that the Church's role is to be a sacrament of this universal presence sounds naively optimistic—as if everything in the garden is just perfect, apart from needing recognition. The fact is that the process of revelation, of shedding light on what is obscure, shows up not only the Godliness latent in all but also the presence of evil. Light reveals both colour and dark shade. This is why for many Christians, as their faith matures, they cease to feel at ease and comfortable with many pursuits which hitherto they regarded as insignificant. Indeed the sense of peace and well-being provided by the well-being of our rather pampered society turn in to something of a sick joke. 'In the world you will no longer have peace, but . . . '.

As the Christian discovers there is no abiding city, and the world is full of comfortable illusions, so the Church's task as sacrament of God's kingdom turns out to have a perverse character as well as a harmonious one. It is the realisation of God's goodness which reveals the full extent of evil and the dire necessity of redemption. It also reveals the critical nature of our ambiguous human condition, bringing an urgency where contentment is easy. 'This may be a wicked age, but your lives should redeem it' (Eph. 5).

Christian faith and praxis is indeed perverse. It seeks to alleviate poverty while saying the Kingdom belongs to the poor. It seeks to alleviate suffering while saying (in the teeth of contemporary ideas of suffering which see it merely as evil to be removed) that suffering yet has redemptive power. It seeks to prevent death while saying (in the teeth of a society which really wants to know nothing about death and the dying) that death is a person's greatest moment of truth.

Above all, perhaps, it knows how to celebrate with festive joy even while engaging seriously in the struggle. Too often a moral seriousness takes command of those involved in social caring or radical politics. This seriousness destroys a sense of beauty and of joy and easily leads to grim dogmatism on the one hand, or despair on the other. But Christian faith, unless it goes awry and offers no more than an opium to people, can celebrate authentic hope because it knows how to engage seriously but to live through failure. It is not buoyed up by a need for instant success, nor by the false expectation of bringing about some worldly utopia. It acts simply because it must act. God's love revealed in Christ urges it.

A Meditation Drawn from Psalms 10 and 37

The Lord sits enthroned for ever
He will judge the world with justice,
judge the peoples with truth.

(But) Lord, why do you stand afar off
and hide yourself in times of distress?
The poor man is devoured by the pride of the wicked
caught in the schemes that others have made.

I have seen the wicked triumphant . . .
I passed by again, he was gone.
The power of the wicked shall be broken
And the Lord will support the just.
The nations have fallen in the pit which they made
. . . snared in the work of their own hands.

Arise Lord, let men not prevail . . .
Let the nations know they are but men.
Arise, Lord, lift up your hand!
O God, do not forget the poor!
The needy shall not always be forgotten
nor the hopes of the poor in vain.

You hear the prayer of the poor
You strengthen their hearts; you turn your ear,
to protect the right of the oppressed
so that mortal man may strike terror no more.

The just man's few possessions
are better than the wicked man's wealth.
The wicked man borrows and cannot repay,
but the just man is generous and gives.

Commit your life to the Lord,
trust in him and he will act.
Be still before the Lord and wait in patience
do not fret at the one who prospers.

Those who do evil shall perish;
the patient shall inherit the land.
The humble shall own the land
and enjoy the fullness of peace.
The just shall inherit the land
there they shall live forever.

The salvation of the just comes from the Lord
The Lord helps them and delivers them
and saves them; their refuge is in him.

(This is not a commentary on these two psalms but some reflections arising from them.)

The Experience of God

It is an old and precious tenet of Catholic spirituality that God's gracious action in us cannot be consciously experienced by us, in itself. We may or may not experience some of its effects, but we cannot be conscious of it, itself. This is because his gracious action does not add an 'extra' on to 'ourselves', but radically transforms our very selves.

When Alice drank the bottle 'Drink Me', the whole of herself changed, she could only know its effects because things around her looked different. Or perhaps it is like a man who unknowingly swallows a tranquiliser or stimulant, and has to infer that that must have happened because he finds his responses are different.

This Catholic tenet has led to a certain shyness over phrases like 'the experience of God' or Protestant doctrines about conviction of 'being saved'. But in recent years this shyness has disappeared, and we talk more happily about the experience of God. In fact in some circles we talk too glibly about it, giving the impression that people are not the real thing unless they experience a certain glow or some felt emotion. That is unfortunate because it leads to false expectations.

Normally, we only know of God's transforming spirit

in and among us when we come to realise that our life has changed – we discover in ourselves a freedom of spirit and a peace, unwarranted by any evidence; we discover a simplifying of outlook and love of truth, unwarranted by what would otherwise be to our own interest; we discover above all a love and concern for people, unwarranted by any human logic. These are the effects of God's gracious transforming power, but to make that inference – that 'the Lord was here and I knew it not' – always requires a certain act of faith which leaves understanding behind.

Our perception of the hand of God in our lives – and in our social history – is therefore a matter of hindsight and a matter of faith. That is, it depends on an act of will and is never self-evident or provable.

What is more, our evolving appreciation of God's creating and redeeming presence comes from and within the practical orientations of our life; it is experiential rather than notional.

When Moses demanded, in his mystical encounter with God, to 'know' his name (for the apologetic reason of getting his oppressed compatriots to take liberation seriously), the reply was really a denial of being able to name and recognise God in that way. Quite what YAHWEH signified has of course been much discussed. But, given the context of the story, I would hazard: I was the God with your fathers, Abraham, Isaac, Joseph; I am the God who likewise will be present to you in your obedience to what I command; you will 'know me' in that obedience. I am the living God.

In other words, we recognise God by hindsight, by recovering the memory, and we know him within our obedience and praxis, as experiential and non-theoretical as the knowledge of lovers.

Jesus said: 'If you love me, keep my commands, and then my father will come . . . ' And St. Paul seems to say to the Romans (Rom 12.2) that only in the process of conforming their lives to the mind of Christ, and non-conforming them to the ways of the world, will they come to perceive what is God's will for them.

God of History

It is a fairly trite truism to say that 'all history is interpreted history'. Anyone knows it who has read both the *Telegraph* and the *Morning Star* on a strike dispute, or has discussed with a colleague, after some committee meeting, just what was said and decided.

Our ability to perceive the real significance of any 'event' depends on our depth of perception, the extent to which our poverty of spirit gives us ears and eyes free of self-interest ('let those who can hear, hear . . . '), and, usually, the passage of time so that hindsight can locate the 'event' in its true context.

By and large scripture perceives the hand of God in history with the hindsight of faith. And this can often mislead us because the accounts seem to be saying, 'The Lord was there and they knew it', rather than 'The Lord was there and they knew it not'. Are we not tempted to a certain pique? If God was there then, why isn't he here now? If God was our help in ages past, why is he not our help in ages present?

For the last few years I have been involved in a small and precarious community. Recently it has all but collapsed and there seem to be two ways of deciding about the future. One is to sit down and work out whether, after our troubled history, there is any foreseeable future. If not, let's cheerfully pack our bags and go home. The other is to remember that four years ago we could not foresee what could come of it, but that during those four years God has blessed us in unpredictable and often quirky ways. All sorts of things happening along, people turning up unexpectedly, and many unwarranted affirmations and signs. If we could not foresee then what blessings (including hardships) were to follow, what right have we now to demand a foreseeable future? By recovering our memory of the past, and with hindsight learning to see the hand of God in it (not self-evident at the time) we learn to have faith in God's presence today and move into the future unprogrammed and free of preconceived models or ideology.

That seems to be how scripture views history, making anamnesis of the past with the hindsight of faith and so learning to have faith in the present, transcending secular interpretations of events which imprison the possible in categories of human logic. It was especially the prophets who had the task of recovering the past, the God of our Fathers, to interpret the future and lift people's vision out of the confines of contemporary secular ideas. In good times they had to warn that the basis on which all seemed well was fickle and illusory. In hard times, when things fell apart, they had to recover the memory of a God who is faithful and draws life out of death.

I think that Jesus came to realise his Father in this way. Formed, in head and heart, by the Law, the Prophets and the Psalms, he interpreted the present experience of his people in these categories of faith in a living God. There seems no reason to think that

Jesus was obedient to the will of his Father in some hot-line, instant memos way. His clarity and assurance came from long hours of pondering and prayer, not from instant orders. That assurance which comes from the power of the Spirit, speaking to our spirit, but does not release us from the ambiguities and complexities of our daily scene.

God of our history

If we are to recover the art of interpreting our contemporary history, not as the sad secular surround to our private spiritual lives but as the significant locus of God's presence—if we are to recover this there are certain scriptural assumptions we need to recover also:

a) God is author in bad times as well as good

God did not only send Moses to liberate his people. It was also God who hardened Pharaoh's heart against Moses.

Nor was it simply God who blessed Job, with family, flocks and land, and Satan who took them away. It was God himself who is said (at the end of the book) to have afflicted Job. The Lord gives. The Lord takes away.

Likewise in many psalms affliction is spoken of as God's doing.

God is not a God simply of blessings and well-being, though we treat him so. He is God of the whole of life. And more often than not our own kingdoms have to fall apart to provide the context for his to emerge.

Jon Sobrino, asked recently whether we in this

country could learn the liberating good news as he and the poor in El Salvador were learning it, simply said: not yet, you have not yet suffered enough.

b) God is author in human's responsibility

God creates people as absolutely responsible for their own history (that is clear in the story of Adam and Eve, and right through the history of God's people), and yet history is the locus of God's will and liberating power (his word does not return without fulfilling his ends). Two sides to the profound mystery of how God's dominion and compassion are total, yet never by-pass human freedom and responsibility.

We can only live in this mystery, never comprehend it. But it certainly forbids any sense of fate or of being the innocent victims of external forces outside human history.

It was for instance very important for the psalmist's faith that nations fell into pits *which they themselves had made,* and that the poor man is *caught in schemes of human making.* Without this sense of human responsibility there is no humility, no repentance, and no liberating future. Only an endless round of manoeuvring and manipulating by those able to do it.

One way we constantly evade human responsibility is by saying that things happen rather than that people do them. I used to chuckle at boys in Math classes who would say 'Sir, I think the question's gone wrong' instead of 'I've messed up the answer'. A youthful evasion which forecasts bigger evasions later on.

Not long before he died, Schumacher wrote an article on inflation in which he pointed to the danger of phrases such as 'Inflation is when prices rise', or

'Inflation is when the value of money falls'. Both phrases ignore human involvement and give the impression that we are all victims of abstract economic law. Just as Jesus warned of the danger of making 'the Law' or 'the Sabbath' into absolutes and subjecting people to them, so monetarists make 'Money', and most of us make 'Economics', into absolutes.

Schumacher's point was that prices do not 'go up', they are 'put up'. Put up by people wanting to cover their costs when their suppliers charge more, and to preserve their income, their standard of living and the differentials they are used to.

'When substantial groups of producers who had previously been considered powerless . . . discover and use their bargaining power, they put up the prices they charge for their goods and services simply in order to obtain a bigger share of the cake. It is, technically, correct to say that the resultant rise in prices, called inflation, is due to their action. From their own point of view, however, whether they be dustmen or OPEC, the cause of inflation is quite different: it is the ruthless determination of others to defend their own incomes by passing on higher costs and insisting on the maintenance of previously established relativities.

'The rich have always been reluctant to acknowledge that bargaining power is the principal factor in the determination of income distribution, that people without power have to be content with small incomes and people with a lot of power can hold out for high incomes.

'. . . Although the present situation lends itself to ruthless exploitation, it cannot be doubted that it stems from the neglect of social justice in the past—

both internally and internationally ... Until we concern ourselves seriously with social and economic justice, we shall find it impossible to conquer the problem of inflation'.

That is one example in our day of a theme essential to the Good News in the New Testament: a call to people in every walk of life to overcome a sense of being pawns in the movements of abstract history and external forces, to recognise that people make history, and, through the humility and metanoia that that recognition demands, to enable their full potential and imagination and creativity (which is the power of God) to take hold of life.

c) The eyes of God are the eyes of the poor

Another scriptural assumption we need to recover, in learning to discover our history as the locus of God's redemptive power, is that the only understanding of history that is real is that seen through the eyes of the poor.

Anyone whose prayer makes much use of the psalms cannot but be struck and challenged by this. But I do not agree that that means only the poor can do real theology and real politics. For one thing, the moral subservience that is so often created in people treated as marginal makes it very unlikely that such theology can spring from there alone. For another, I do not think that Jesus himself was one of the poor, in the sense of being marginalised (and so made to feel guilty) by the conditions of his life. He came from a fairly secure, artisan background. His poverty was that of deliberate choice to identify with the poor, a deliberate choice to drive in the slow lane not the fast one, as it were.

You who read this are more than likely well-educated and more or less middle class. You may fear that you are thereby condemned to seeing all things with bourgeois eyes, because you can never share in the memories and insecurities and feelings of being at fault, which characterise the poor. But although we are conditioned by our upbringing we are never determined by it. We also have a uniquely human/divine ability to transcend our conditioning not only to know things a particular way, but also to know how and why we know thus. In other words, given the necessary orientations and options in life, we can come to see—at least partially—with the eyes of others.

In the amazing evolution of basic Christian communities in Latin America it is not true that life and hope have come simply 'from below'. They have come from the interplay and involvements not only of the dispossessed but of theologians, bishops, priests, sisters, educated and professional people, intent on making their specific contribution and learning from the poor themselves how to read history through their eyes and to engage from their stand point.

d) God's love for his people

Finally, I think we need to recover a faith in God as redeemer of a people in their history.

There is a cry in one of the psalms that always makes me ponder: Remember me, Lord, out of the love you have for your people. I find it challenges me because there is so little in my mental make-up which can appreciate that a people as such, in all its historical reality, political structures, shared outlooks and actions, can—as such—be a locus of God's redemptive, liberating power. Everything else in me prays: Lord remember your people out of the love you have for its members. But here I pray: Remember, and save me, as a participating member of a people whom you love and redeem.

St. Paul's perception of the Church as being the Body of Christ sends me pondering along the same lines. It is absurd to suppose that any member of a Body, eye, hand, foot, heart, can become what it is called to be except in its participation in the redemption of the Body.

And if the Church is sacrament of God's redemptive work in the world at large, what we can apprehend in a coherent way of the Church we need to apprehend in an incoherent way of the world at large.

Many people today have a real sense of guilt from being part of a society whose whole fabric is unjust. This guilt is often a destructive one, eating into their consciousness because it is devoid of any redemptive hope. But God is not interested in people building up a collective guilt complex simply in order to feel awful. God only reveals guilt, and sin, to us in the context of redemptive love. And if we recover a scriptural faith in God's love for a people, as such, in its real history, then we could also cope with an awareness of corporate sin—an awareness which alone can call to corporate 'metanoia', the pre-condition of redemption.

In his book *The Politics of Jesus,* John Howard Yoder discusses Paul's understanding of social structures and political power. He reminds the reader that the scriptural attitude to all created things is not that they are simply good or simply bad. (God alone is the former, and nothing could be created which was the latter!) Scriptural faith, and traditional Christian faith, is that all things are created good (in their essential being they are good), that all things are fallen (fallen apart and alienated as a result of and a cause of sin), and that all things are being redeemed. And this applies not only to the individual as a locus of God's grace – in fact it does not apply there anything like as much as we have thought – but also to the corporate whole.

The understanding of the economy of redemption forbids any naive analysis of political structures as being simply good or simply bad, and it forbids any expectation of a perfect utopia this side of the great consummation, when God shall be all in all. But it does demand a radical, serious appreciation of our political, social, history and that we are redeemed through incorporation into God's love for his people.

CHAPTER FIVE

Eucharist and Politics

Introduction

OURS is a moment in history of great bewilderment; we are baffled by the never-ending social issues that are thrust at us and often we have not the mental categories or emotional maturity with which to interpret them. Bafflement always leads either to apathy and despair or to an emptying of self and renewal in God. And renewal in the Church has always taken the path either of exciting new enthusiasms along the peripheries of faith (which end up as being quite irrelevant) or of a return to the central mystery of Christianity to ask new questions there.

So it will be useful to consider the Eucharist because we have there the fullest, the consummate expression of the Church's faith. If we ask what is the specific character of the Christian concern for people we must be able to find the answer in the Eucharist.

It is familiar to all who have 'done theology' that the Eucharist is a threefold sign of the past, of the present, and of the future: a sign of Christ's passover for us in AD30, a sign of our present reconciliation to and communion with him and one another, and a pledge of our final union in the kingdom. Christ has died, is risen, will come. But what has not been stressed, because of its protestant overtones for the last 400 years, is that the Eucharist is also a sign of our faith, a *signum fidei,* not only a sign of God's initiative on our behalf, but also a sign of our 'yes' in response. The Eucharist makes clear and explicit our inner response of faith, not a merely private and cosy 'yes', but a public and communal commitment to fundamental attitudes arising from God's initiative on our behalf, fundamental attitudes of mind about what it is to be human.

Most Christians know the tension between a personalist god-and-me-concerned-about-my-salvation type of faith, and a God-can-only-be-found-in-my-neighbour type of faith. They know this tension within themselves, or at least as a tension between different types of people. In recent years there has been a move away from a vertical faith centred on 'me and God' towards a horizontal faith centred on social awareness. This movement makes the tension acute, especially for many priests, many of whom are bewildered by the contrast between the personal devotion approach of their background and the demands to get socially involved which they meet on all sides today.

To be content with either a vertical personalist faith or a horizontal socialist faith is to deny the Incarnation. It would be easy to try to integrate the two, as is often done in Christian social writing, by presenting as Christian thought what is really only dolled-up humanism interspersed with apt gospel quotations. But God is not to be a helpmate for our frenetic social activism, and the following considerations are an attempt to integrate the two aspects, personal and social, without falling into that trap.

Human beings are political, in the sense that their daily position is never in isolation but always set within an intricate web of social structures. To answer the question 'who am I' is to study the whole setting in which my life is set up and has its purpose. In this sense my life is political; I am involved in politics.

Politics can be taken to mean formal politics (parties or organisations), or real politics (principles and ground-work of human inter-relations). Here we are concerned with real politics, and in that sense we can say that the Eucharist is a radical political statement about man. Far from being a sabbath day escape from the world, it is a fundamental political stance within it. It is celebrated on the first day of the week, not the last. In the Eucharist we find ourselves caught up into Christ in his return to the Father. Our aspirations and concern are brought into the aspirations of God himself. We learn to see as God sees, not from a borrowed principle outside ourself, but from our own heightened awareness.

So week by week we make, in the Eucharist, our political statement. The problem is to become aware of the implications of that statement. To do so it may help us to consider five truths to which we say 'yes':

The dignity of man
The freedom of man
The givenness of things
The power of life and love over death and hatred
The love of people springs from experience of God.

The Dignity of Man

The chaotic jumble of people coming to communion in our large churches is a good statement of what it is all about. A total disregard for status, colour, income, no sense of 'them' and 'us'. Indeed, Christ does not present to us his body, nor even his body given for us, but his body given for us to be eaten together; the together is an essential part of the sign and the communion.

The 'dignity of man' is hardly understood in terms of individual rights over against others (as in the Declaration of Human Rights). Rather does it lie in man's elevation to be sons and daughters of God by virtue of Christ's being son of God.

The Eucharist reveals to us the real dignity of man, which would otherwise be unknown to us; and it establishes the source of this dignity which is that man is not only created in the image of God but has also been reconciled as son or daughter of God from a radical alienation which none but God could get to the root of. The immediate consequence, in fact the actual realisation of this is concern for reconciliation among people.

Most Christians think too much of love in terms of doing good, of helping the poor, of giving money. Just below the surface is a sense of salving one's conscience, or even a sense of 'achievement'. But love begins in the heart of God, and our concern for people can never be other than our gratitude for love received. 'If we would know whether God's love has really taken hold in us, then we must ask: do we find ourselves loving our brethren?'

Now love to be true must be efficacious, and to be

efficacious it must go beyond mere charity to a mature sense of justice. The distinction is vital. It used, for instance, to be thought that most problems between rich countries and poor countries could be solved by 'aid' and by sufficient money given to 'charities'. In other words, where there is sufficient good will there is a way, and what is needed are dozens of Mother Teresas. But this is not true; we know that the root causes of destitution, homelessness, unemployment and hunger in the world are not the lack of charity and good will, but the lack of justice. And justice is to do with objective relationships and structures. This is why it is naive to talk of cunning capitalist and colonialist plots against the innocent poor. It is perfectly possible for good people to be in unjust situations, and for evil people to be in just ones. The problem is not one of malice; it is one of blindness.

This seems to be the central thrust of Christ's warnings to those in power or with riches. Not a condemnation, but a very dire warning that power and riches create blindness; an urgent call, for their own sake, to be aware.

When a supermarket arrives in a High Street and sees the local grocer do worse and worse month by month, it is relatively easy for it to be concerned and offer help, to be kind; what it is almost impossible for it to admit is that its own presence and growth and establishment is the root cause of the grocer's decline and hopeless future. This is almost exactly the psychology of our relationship with the third world. As long as concern for Christ's brothers and sisters is one of charity and kindness we are all for it, but when that concern develops into an awareness of justice the whole issue becomes awkward.

It is now becoming more and more clear that affluence and poverty do not just 'happen', and also that the 'trickle down' theory—that wealth earned by some is bound to spread to all—is erroneous. What is being realised is that the same processes that create wealth or power for some, also create poverty or powerlessness for others. A small microcosm example illustrates this: our local bus service has recently closed; we were distressed for the old people in the village who cannot get about, were anxious to help with our vehicles, and to encourage alternative transport arrangements. But what is extremely difficult to acknowledge is that it was precisely our use of private cars which killed the bus service, that we are part of the actual process.

In this country, in general, there is a polarising process going on between the wealthy and the destitute. The growth of the urban poor, the rising number of families on social welfare, spell out the same message: that a society bent on acquiring affluence must work to benefit those who are well off and it will do this both through educating people's attitudes and through its own economic structures. And this same process operates between nations, so that to think of rich-poor in terms of charity, or of 'them sooner or later catching up with us', has become a form of social blindness. It is essential that the Church lays bare these issues with the same urgency with which Christ warned those in positions of power in Palestine.

One of the root causes of injustice in society is the psychological or physical distance between those who make decisions and those affected by them. It is no accident that unemployment increases as one goes north from offices in London to workers in Liverpool or Glasgow, or that a profound sense of 'them', the southerners, exploiting 'us' in Durham, say, still lingers from the thirties. The same factors operate wherever there is lack of genuine sympathy-born-of-experience between those who decide and those who are affected, whether in a family, in the Church, or between nations. To counter this it is necessary to free ourselves from familiar categories of thinking in terms of 'them' and 'us', and this freeing is as much a question of having a feel for the dignity of every person as it is of acknowledging it nationally. It is a question of appreciating at a radical level what it means that God shared his life with people rather than just helping them from a distance.

This sense of integration would have colossal political implications, not only within our own country but internationally. I am, after all, as closely bound to the Bolivian tin miner who initiates the tin coating on my Nescafe tin this morning as I am to the grocer who sold me the tin. Yet the Bolivian is 'them' and the grocer is 'us'. And the Bolivian lives on hunger and injustice (at £7 a month) and the grocer lives affluently. The truth of our world is that it is a global, closely interdependent village, but our mental attitudes are still along the lines of we-matter-and-they-should-struggle-for-themselves.

We need to receive in the Body of Christ a thirst for justice, for reconciliation, for a sense of the dignity of every person, in order that he can use us in our own spheres of life as a voice for the voiceless and a 'contestator' of the established structures of injustice. This above all is asked of priests.

The Freedom of Man

There is a certain embarrassment among Catholics because we have suddenly realised, at a time when all the world is interested in freedom, that that is precisely what we were meant to be interested in all along, in spite of our emphases on obedience and acceptance. A little like having to search through a wastepaper basket for a letter one has realised is very important.

In the Eucharist we celebrate the passover of Christ from the total unfreedom of death to his transcendent freedom as Son of God. In that celebration we not only state, but discover the possibility of, the freedom which God offers to every person.

The whole history of God's people can be taken as a continuous call by God to a freedom which his people over and over could not take, a call to liberation from what was familiar but unworthy of people, to a new freedom with God, which was worthy of them. And throughout the ministry of Jesus we hear the same call. Leave what is familiar and limiting and stand up on your own feet and discover the freedom that I offer to you.

Unfortunately we inherit two attitudes that prevent us from having a mature understanding of freedom. The first is that freedom is mainly a question of having shackles removed, of other people getting off one's back. This is to equate freedom with independence, whereas in fact freedom is an inner ability to take responsibility for one's own future, to be the author of one's own destiny.

Freedom, both for the individual or for a society or nation at large, is not something that happens—for instance when 'independence' is gained; rather it is built up and nurtured over many years. The maturing of freedom, either within a personality or a society, is something which makes great demands on people and calls for great sacrifices. Perhaps it is this long haul, this need for 'patient endurance', which contemporary man finds so distasteful but which the New Testament equates with hope and faith.

The second attitude which inhibits our understanding of freedom is that freedom is about the rights of an individual over against his society, or a nation over against the rest of the world. This outlook arises from the western protestant emphasis on man as an individual. It lies behind our naive ideas of human rights (as residing in man's self rather than in relationships with others). It lies behind our worship of doing our own thing, of getting on in the world, of doing well for oneself. It lies behind the whole competitive assumption that the human quality of life is best secured by a free interplay of human competition. Those two beautiful words 'free' and 'enterprise', which should refer to the very highest in man, to be free and to be creative, have turned into symbols of oppression for most people alive in our present world. Free enterprise based on individual competition at the expense of concern for people must inevitably oppress.

We tend to interpret the underdevelopment of the poor countries in terms of economics or of politics. More basic than either of these is the state of moral depression which removes any desire in the poor or powerless to transcend their condition. This is unfreedom in its ultimate form, the psychological state of total dependence on a system which oppresses. This is total alienation, in that people's energies go into work that does not make them in any sense authors of their own destiny. They are working for a 'them' and not for an 'us'. This is the root cause of much poverty in the world, particularly in Latin America. It is not possible for an elite within a country, or a foreign power outside it, to pursue the basic tenets of our western economics without building up profound moral lassitude, unfreedom and alienation in millions of people.

The cure being adopted more and more widely by those aware of what has happened is to start right at the base to educate people in awareness, to be aware of their situation, aware of what their life is about, its organisation, its possibilities, aware above all that what their parents assumed to be permanent their children should know can be otherwise. As Paulo Freire has said: 'We do not want to be the object of civilisation but the subject of civilisation'. In his letter to the UNCTAD III meeting in April 1972 Pope Paul emphasised that not all the reordering of trade terms and monetary systems and overseas aid would do justice to the third world unless those countries themselves became part of the decision-making structure.

In our own country we find a similar moral underdevelopment created by our welfare thinking and by our assumption that higher wages and pensions and handouts are the main issues for governments and trade unions. The tragedy of unemployment is not financial, it is that society is telling a person 'we can get on without you. And I'm afraid at present we're too busy to find you a creative part'.

It is too easy to think in terms of the affluent being free and the poor being in need of liberation. If anything in the gospels Jesus is more concerned to liberate the affluent than the oppressed. And our contemporary issues of international injustice are far more a call from God to liberate the affluent than they are to liberate the poor; it seems that there is no solution to the deepest problems of the poorer nations apart from a genuine liberation of the wealthy from their own economic assumptions.

It is likewise becoming clear to the Church in the West that the inner renewal we look for cannot be found at the rather superficial levels we have been hoping for, but only at the more devastating level of bringing Jesus' call to liberation and to poverty to bear in our sophisticated world. We need to apply theological wisdom to social structures and attitudes.

The Giveness of Things

Eucharist means thanksgiving, gratitude, appreciation, a total response to God for receiving all things at his hands. We cannot celebrate the Eucharist out of context with our total attitude to possessions and ownership.

The Eucharist is also an explicit denial of any form of dualism: that material things don't matter, that it is the spirit alone that is relevant. God presents himself to us as things, things to be eaten and to be drunk. This is incarnation in its full expression and should be a dire warning against making Christian faith 'spiritual', of thinking for instance that Jesus was really talking about being poor in spirit in a way that makes no demands on our life style.

When poverty is talked about, people immediately think of St. Francis. In general we have inherited quite a developed theology and tradition of giving everything up for the freedom of the kingdom – even if few of us are any good at doing so, and even if more of us are probably called to that total handing over than in fact ever have a go. But to complement that poverty of go-sell-give-come-follow we also need a theology of ownership (which we have not at all inherited). Most people are in no position to relinquish all, because of family and other responsibilities. But all of us need to theologise contemplatively on: what does it mean for me to *own* this car, this house, to *have* this talent, this skill, to be able to enjoy and indulge in so many things?

The highest response of which we are capable is that of pure wonder and awe and appreciation and gratitude for what we enjoy. This is not a theoretical, idealised appreciation; it refers to concrete day to day things and money and talents. It is not a back to nature appreciation which finds it easy to appreciate mountains and trees, but almost impossible to appreciate and give thanks for computers and cars. It is easy to build up a dark sense of guilt about what is enjoyed in a sophisticated developed world, so that concern for the destitute is based on guilt and not gratitude. But gratitude is the authentic Christian response. It is gratitude that gives a lightness of touch towards things, which insists that 'possession' is relative not absolute, and which insists that all private ownership presupposes a communal one. Because things and abilities and intelligence and money and property are fundamentally 'received' rather than 'earned' and because they are received at the hands of God by an individual primarily for the sake of all his sons and daughters and not exclusively to be 'possessed', the immediate expression of gratitude is a desire to share. The authentic Christian response is gratitude not guilt, and a desire to share rather than to give. Sharing carries the hint of giving what already belongs to another or at least what is equally owned by anyone. It carries no hint of superiority nor any pat on the back for doing good.

In the writings of the Fathers, of Thomas Aquinas, and more recently in *Gaudium et Spes* and *Populorum Progressio,* there is a strong tradition of Christian thought along these lines. This tradition, this intuitive sense about what it means to own things or to hold power in one's hands, needs to be seen clearly, today, worked out in the practical judgements and the life-styles of Christians and of the Church.

One immediate application of such an understanding of ownership, which is increasingly important in international justice, is the question of natural resources – their use and who benefits from their exploitation. And another is how the massive inherited benefits and power of our own rich world can be used for the genuine good of all.

It would be naive to base a theology of ownership simply on the positive need for a sincere attitude of gratitude. We also need a contemporary assessment of what it meant for Christ to take on not the role of the powerful, of the political leader, of the owner, of the person whose wealth or position enables one to do much charitable good for those in need, but rather the role of the dispossessed, the powerless, the poor. That he chose this quite deliberately is clear from the gospels in his refusal to accept political leadership and his determination to see this association with the weak and the vulnerable through to the end (and it led to his death). This is what Paul refers to in saying that Christ did not cling to what was his by right but dispossessed himself. He took the role of one neglected and despised and rejected. There are many aspects of Christ's non-violent and vulnerable association with the poor. There is, for instance, the position he took in contrast to Barabbas. Barabbas was more or less a guerilla fighter seeking solutions to injustice which Christ himself had rejected and which were in fact less dangerous and seditious than the vulnerable approach chosen by Christ; that is why the leaders chose Barabbas. Again Christ was certainly tempted to make use, for excellent ends, of the power that was his for the asking, and the significance of his threefold temptation in the desert must be quite clear to anyone who understands questions of international justice and development today. The insidious temptation to use wealth or power to produce food or material prosperity at the expense of higher spiritual and cultural values (man really does not live by bread alone); the temptation to use demonstrations of power or status to win people or nations; the temptation to control the whole world at the expense of its and our own true freedom to God—these are by no means outdated in our own day. Unfortunately not enough of us ever withdraw into the desert in order to see these for the temptations which they are and the roots of injustice.

Perhaps the greatest need for the western world is to grow out of its sense of superiority and learn humbly to get off the backs of other nations. As Christians we need to learn that Christ did not come to help the poor, he became one of them; it was not a question of pity or of Christ's being God's gift to the wretched, but a question of the poor being the ones, after all, who really mattered. The kingdom was to belong to these, and those with power or riches would find it desperately hard to enter. This was not because they would be refused but because power and riches involve concern for ever more material affairs and a consequent blindness which precludes them from appreciating the real issues at stake, from ever hearing God's call to freedom, and to life, which is the 'kingdom'.

Jesus did not accuse the rich of malice; he warned them of blindness, of having ears that simply couldn't hear and eyes that couldn't see. What would cut people off from the kingdom was not, after all, sin but it was good things—buying a farm, getting married, buying oxen (or a car). It was the clutter of good things which would pre-occupy their hearts and heads. Jesus made this clear in the language of a prophet, one who is dealing with an issue that is both critical and ultimate. In this respect the Church's voice needs to be heard as a prophet's voice, the voice that can challenge people to generous decisions, that can elicit the ultimate good in people. And of course this voice is far less the spoken word than the living image presented by the Church and her members.

In particular this presenting anew of Christ's warnings needs to make quite clear that nations or classes of people and people of goodwill (ourselves and our friends) can be upholders of situations of injustice which they themselves have not chosen.

For people to discover this—and it must be a painful and demanding discovery—is the first liberation for the affluent or the powerful.

The Power of Life and Love

It is often urged that Sunday Mass should be used to get over to people the urgency of international injustice and poverty in the world. The homily and bidding prayers are to be used as God-given teaching platforms. But it is the whole celebration of mass which leads us into the heart of human suffering and injustice and life and joy and peace. We celebrate the Paschal Mystery of Christ and in that celebration acknowledge that the forces of love and reconciliation in the world are more powerful than the forces of evil and injustice. This is not a pious memento of an event over and done with two thousand years ago, nor is it naive wishful thinking about another world hence; it is an act of faith about the concrete historical world in which we live. He who was a failure, who was rejected by men, was raised to life by God. His death was not a hero's triumph, it was not a Pelagian achievement, he was not a 'martyr to self'. Jesus Christ Superstar is quite wrong.

Man's ways are not God's ways, and the mystery of Christ's cross and his subsequent resurrection can only be understood in the language of faith. But it is nevertheless the archetype of God's whole command of the world. The failure and rejection of Jesus was precisely that through which God liberated his people. Christians cannot be content with a humanism that sees suffering simply as evil. Christ has triumphed, God has not lost control of his own world, neither over-all nor in detail. All really will be well.

There are two opposite poles in this, both of which have to be held at the same time. First, there is profound social injustice in the world; it is of a critical nature, and God's invitation to an effective and vigorous response is real. Second, whatever the degree of human misery and injustice, and however absent God may seem to be, yet he is present, and will indeed turn all things to good. These two faces of the mystery cannot be grasped together; they can only be lived and not expounded, and they can be seen most clearly in the serene peace of mind found in those deeply involved in serving the destitute in Christ. We like to think that God raised Jesus in spite of his passion and death, but in fact he was raised because of it; his new life emerged through his death and God will achieve his purpose in the world not in spite of the mess but through and within it. The death of the seed in the ground is one and the same movement as its growth to life and fruition.

Christian hope is never naive wishful thinking; it always takes the mess seriously. But it does not become so agonised by sheer impotence when faced, say, by the structural injustice and sin of our own society, that it ceases to 'find a way'. Christ was not a solver of social problems and we do not expect easy answers to the mess; but he does show us how to live within the mess; he does show us the power of patience; and he does give us the vision which shatters the conventional (and at present quite baffled) ways of interpreting the mess.

Love of People is from God

The final political statement to which we say 'yes' in the Eucharist is that our concern for man springs from our experience of God, or, as St. John put it, it is the love of God in us which enables us to love our brother in need. There is a tendency today to reduce the gospel to social activity, a tendency to think of humanists, communists, and Christians as all doing the same basic thing, but the last as having some sort of overdrive which should make it clear to everyone that they can do good better than others.

But Christian faith is grounded in our experience of God, our encounter with God, and this is not 'for' anything. It is not to enable us to love each other more. When we experience moments of great beauty, moments which take us out of ourselves, such appreciation is its own end, its own justification. So it is with our experience of God and we must be able to say, with St. Peter, on the mount of Transfiguration, 'It is simply good for us to be here' full stop. It is only then that Christian ethics have meaning. Otherwise we submit God to humanity; we use his presence and don't enjoy it. Until we know that there is a good beyond the ethical, the ethical itself is groundless.

Communion in the first place, therefore, is not for peace, or for freedom, or for anything; in the first place it is for itself, communion with our God. And we say all glory and honour are his, Amen, full stop. It is only then that the social involvement of the Church and the believer makes sense. But of course it makes far greater sense because of this subordination to the divine encounter than if we attempt an independent social concern centred only on 'man' as self-contained. Man can only arrive at mature freedom, at personal dignity, at complete reconciliation with fellow men and women, when in union with God. This is because man's whole being is open-ended towards communion with God, and he is necessarily immature until that communion. This is not a pious nicety for believers, but a basic statement about what people, ordinary people, three thousand million people, are all about.

The immediate consequence, politically, is that no 'system' will ensure what man most deeply hungers for. It will never be 'satisfactory'. We have already mentioned that human freedom can never be ensured by any formal politics, however essential it may be to struggle for those political structures which most enhance people's inner freedom and least encourage greed and competition. But political structures are necessarily unsatisfactory, not because they are merely provisional until the real kingdom of heaven (as early Christians thought), but because they have to do with the conditions in which man lives, not ultimately with life itself. This is not to underplay the fact that the way people are treated is what they become, that social and economic structures can, as Marx made clear, condition people to be alienated from themselves and from their brothers and sisters. Indeed, it is this alienation within a consumer and affluent society which will prove our saddest legacy to the emerging nations.

But Marx's accusation that religion alienates man because it places man's real self not in the here and now political reality, but in some other-worldly religious sphere, is only valid given a world view that is non-incarnational. This view (which Marx met in Christians) interprets the world as a massive and dangerous ambush, with religion, faith, prayer as the only secure and saving flight from the world. Today we need, rather, a world view that deeply appreciates the world as God's creation, and a faith that discovers in prayer and the experience of God the full dignity and importance of people. We shall then discover that real politics and justice and social concern matter more than we ever realised, because man has an essential openness to communion with God and, in that communion, to his brothers and sisters. It is this very openness which is hindered and blocked by our failure to take the here and now tragedy of man seriously.

CHAPTER SIX

Hope and Expectation: How We Live the Story

HE was into Zen decades before it became fashionable. And by now his Buddhist spirituality and Christian faith were integrated and as natural to him as the air he breathed. But my hackles were up because he was lecturing me on how mistaken was the current emphasis on 'hope' to be found in so many theologians and spiritual writers today. It was, he said, a lethal distraction from all sound spirituality which must focus on the art of living totally and peacefully in acceptance of the present moment. We must incarnate in our daily life, here and now, the eternal 'nunc stans' of God.

It was not a conversation. That was why my hackles were up. I sensed a slippage of language. I was agreeing and disagreeing but there was no opening for discussion as the benign lecture went on. So my mind went off and alighted on one of those crucial distinctions which had meant so much to me when I first met it. A distinction which had opened up great areas of understanding.

It was the distinction between living in expectation and living in hope. Expectation is the projection into the future of what one knows about at present. It envisages the possibilities of the future either in terms of what one recalls from the past or of what one knows as possible in the present. It will cling to known ways and will plan, worry and manipulate in order to secure these (or achieve them) in the future. Its vision of God will be of one who 'restores fortunes to Israel', delivers the goods, prolongs well being, and answers prayers as prayed.

Hope, on the other hand, liberates from expectation. It is centred in the endlessly creative power of God to generate new things, to draw life out of death, to transcend our conditioned minds and generate a future created more by our imaginative and creative powers than by programmes and planning.

To live in hope, rather than expectation, is in fact to live wholly in the present moment. It is to look to the future as unexpected gift, knowing that one is only an instrument in the creation of that gift to the extent that one is fully alive to the present.

In many ways the story of the apostles given in the gospels is a story of hope breaking through the confines of expectations—from the time when they realised that Jesus was the one who had been 'waited for', until the break through, at Pentecost, when they realised God as creator of the unexpected. It was a constant and painful dying of their expectations of the Messiah, and of how God ought to do things, to a liberation from all constraining ideas and criteria. It is not easy for us to appreciate how they experienced the crucifixion as the collapse of all their expectations, though one senses it keenly in some of the Easter stories. One feels the pathos in Luke's story of the two disciples on the road to Emmaus telling their anonymous hitchhiker how, after all that Jesus had taught and done, they really expected him to have redeemed Israel. But all had collapsed in his death. And then the awakening, as their hearts burned within them, of resurrection-hope, confirmed in the breaking of bread.

The cross-resurrection of Jesus is the paradigm not only of liturgical worship and abstract theology. It is the paradigm for interpreting the daily experience of life, personal and political. If spiritual writers down through the ages have focussed on the personal, there is today a great hunger for the political—an interpretation of our history that will provide criteria for social and political discernment and option.

We live, at the present time, under the shadow of a terrible spectre: fascism. Whether it be the overt fascism of ultra left or ultra right wing regimes (it matters not) —Russia, South Africa, Latin American juntas—or the benign, and in some ways more insidious fascism of America or Britain.

I have recently been reading a biography of Archbishop Romero (killed, just two years ago, in San Salvador, by a bullet through the heart while saying Mass). His life, and his death, clarify a basic political option which lies before each of us in one form or another. When he was first a bishop his focus was on prayer and personal conversion, thinking as so many Christians do that politics would look after itself as long as people lead personally good and honest lives. But the brutal events of his country and the emerging vitality of base-communities among the poor realigned his whole stance.

He came to see that the real story of a people is not written by the manipulations and coercions of those in power, ready to sacrifice people to economic theory and national security. It is written by the emerging hope and involvement of the poor.

In that basic option lies a deep act of faith, because it refuses to use power and policy to strengthen economic processes if those processes are at the expense of people. And they always are at the expense of people, the most vulnerable people, because economic strength is achieved by flattering the strong not the weak.

I suspect that Isaiah faced exactly the same issues, exactly the same political/economic options. If you 'let the oppressed go free, share your bread, pour yourself out for the hungry, satisfy the desire of the afflicted . . . then shall your light break forth like the dawn, your healing spring up' (Is. 58). He is not talking piety; he is calling to a radical political option. He is calling to an act of faith and hope that the real history of his people would not be written by the expectations of the strong but by the authentic hope of the weak. The role of those in power is not to manipulate but to enable.

CHAPTER SEVEN

Reliving the Memory: Making Anamnesis

Listening recently to *Messiah* on the radio, I spent most of parts II and III pondering over the jump between parts I and II. The man who selected the texts for Handel took it as quite natural that part I should dwell on Christ's nativity and that part II should move straight to his death and resurrection.

We make that same jump in most of our communal forms of 'calling to mind' and renewing our faith in Jesus. In the creed he was born of the Virgin Mary—jump—suffered under Pontius Pilate, was crucified . . .

In our Eucharistic prayers we 'make anamnesis', revive the memory, of Jesus in his death, resurrection, ascension, what we call his Paschal Mystery. We do not recall what he did, and preached, and taught during his life.

In fact, when we 'do this in memory' of him, when we keep alive and present the memory of Jesus, we do not recall what *he did,* but only what *happened* to him.

Hardly how we commemorate anyone else whom we love or revere! What does it mean?

1. Why we recall Jesus' death and resurrection

First, recalling what happened to Jesus tells us something about the deep ways of God's action among us. If we acknowledge Christ not simply as an 'other', to be admired as 'other', but as a paradigm of our own lives as we journey into God, then we too discover that God enters and transforms through what happens to us rather than through what we do. God enters through the holes, through the chinks in our armour, through our poverty, our spaces, our silence, our weakness and suffering, through our loss of 'self'. He enters supremely through our death.

This does not mean that what we do is irrelevant. It is no invitation to quietism or the wrong sort of passivity. Nor is it a mystique of failure and suffering.

It does matter what we do, where we place ourselves, in what direction we look, what we consciously believe and pursue and decide and give ourselves to, our political and social stance – all are important. But they are important because they define the holes; they give significance to the spaces, the happenings, the sufferings, as the strings of a net define the holes in the net, or as the notes in music define its silence, because silence can be either empty void or pregnant with meaning, depending on the context.

Of course most of us, when we first become aware of God's calling, set out 'to do God's will'. He is lucky to have us around, and our endeavours on his behalf are mixed up with somewhat Pelagian attitudes. As time goes by God teaches us, by experience, that 'I come to do your will' must give way to 'may your will be done in me'.

This is true even – should I say, most of all? – in our

prayer. In our monastic rule St. Benedict refers to our community round of prayer as *Opus Dei,* the work of God. It took me twenty five years to discover that *Opus Dei* can better be read as the work of God in and among us, rather than our work for God. (Rather as St. John, speaking of the Love of God means God's love for us rather than ours for him.)

One often finds in people who live close to God, and know him as incarnate in the realities of life, a beautiful tension between endeavour and detachment, between decisiveness and waiting, between engagement and withdrawal. Somehow they instinctively know that the kingdom is not what we build on God's behalf, but what 'comes' and what we can 'enter', if the context provided by our active lives enables us to do so.

For Jesus the 'kingdom' is gift and grace, not achievement. The thrust of all his parables of the kingdom was to try and find ways of conveying to those who followed and to those who would not that the kingdom is the work of God's compassion amongst us. The fact that it seems ineffective, frustrated, faintly absurd, is no reason for lack of confidence, perseverance and hope. Indeed, some of the texts which our do-it-yourself Christian inheritance has read as referring to the need for us to be fully effective were originally about God being effective, however unlikely it may seem. When for instance Jesus said, 'No-one lights a lamp simply to hide it under a tin can or in the cellar', he was probably saying 'Do not be over anxious about how and where and when all that I'm talking about will be effective. God has lit the lamp, and he will not have it snuffed out. The lamp's task is to be a good lamp' (almost the opposite of our reading of that reply, as calling on disciples not to 'hide their lamps under a bushel').

Or again Jesus probably meant, by the merchant who sold all to purchase the pearl of great price, that God gives his all to purchase the pearl (you, me, us) hidden in the world's field. He was not talking about our discipleship and abandonment, but of God's total fidelity and determination.

Those of us called to any form of ministry have a modest and enabling task, because however urgent or important our role may seem, the Spirit blows not only where it chooses, but also when and how. And it often blows backwards through the holes we think it is blowing forwards through. How often we find God ministering to us through those who think we are ministering to them. The penitent ministers to the confessor, the counselled to the counsellor, the patient to the doctor. And it is more or less true for all of us that 'we can save others but we cannot save ourselves' —even by the work we do in Christ's name.

In part of his commentary on Charles Williams's Arthurian poems, C.S. Lewis wrote:

> We touch upon one of Williams's fundamental principles. It might be illustrated from the whole history of Judaism and Christianity. Israel is always failing, but there is always a 'remnant' left; out of that failure at its nadir, and that remnant at its smallest, salvation flows . . . For Williams (as we see in 'He Came Down From Heaven') the chosen example is the story of Cain and Abel. Cain has carefully and, no doubt, laudably, prepared an altar and a sacrifice, but no fire descends on it. The fire descends elsewhere, on his brother's altar. Cain fails to under-

stand that this... is one of the laws of the city. 'Unless devotion is given to a thing which must prove false in the end, the thing that is true in the end cannot enter'. 'The way must be made ready for heaven, and then it will come by some other; the sacrifice must be made ready, and the fire will strike on another altar'.

Cain did not understand that 'the very purpose of his offering was to make his brother's acceptable.' And this is what nearly always happens. The thing which we thought principally intended ... comes to nought; what seems to us mere by-product... bursts into flower. Thus to those who wish to stand on their merits, the course of destiny must always seem a horrible celestial sarcasm on their repeated failures: but to those who have been set free by 'the doctrine of largesse' it will be an 'excellent absurdity', a tender mockery dancing or flickering like summer lightning on what, but for this, they might... have regarded as their successes. Once you have grasped the principle, it is not chastening but liberating to know that one has always been almost wholly superfluous; wherever one has done well some other has done all the real work... you will do the same for him, perhaps, another day, but you will not know it—'My friend's shelter for me, mine for him'.

2. The dangers of restricting our recollection to Jesus' death and resurrection

But there are dangers. For many centuries our Western tradition has been used to focussing on the Cross out of the context of Jesus' life as a whole. Many phrases we are used to, such as 'he died to save us from our sins', or 'he died for us and for our salvation', or 'he died in obedience to the will of his Father', carry with them strange connotations of magic. We adhere to them by faith, but some of that faith is a naked belief substituting for understanding, and I think for many of us it goes with misgivings we learn to repress. It is not easy to be critical of long established and loved formulae.

So what are the dangers? First, to extract the Cross from the life of Jesus as a whole makes his sacrifice self-authenticating. It makes out, or at least gives the impression, that the mere fact of his death, in isolation, was somehow pleasing to God, and redemptive.

That is, of course, to fly in the face of all the urgent warnings of the prophets that offering sacrifice is meaningless in itself, because it draws its meaning only from its setting within a life devoted to justice, to compassion for people, and especially for the downtrodden and neglected. Indeed, the prophets went further and warned that sacrifice is not only meaningless apart from its context in life, but that it becomes a counter sign and an insult to God, religiosity converting the things of God into idolatrous God-substitutes.

In his own preaching Jesus had taken up this prophetic tradition and warned of the dangers, for religious people, of treating not only sacrifice but any prayer and any religious practice as self-authenticating.

Intimacy with his Abba-Father, in prayer and religious observance, was in constant dialectic with a hunger and thirst for justice, a consuming compassion for sinners and outcasts, and a singleminded concern for what is true and real in human affairs.

It seems hardly likely that his Abba-God would, at

the end, suddenly become a God who willed the death of his own son as an immolation or satisfaction in its own right.

If we do not grasp this principle, that sacrifice, suffering, death, weakness, holes, are redemptive only by virtue of the over-all context in which they take place, then we pervert the central Christian mystery into a terrible mystique.

Paul refers again and again to the fact that God's power is made perfect in weakness (2 Cor 1 v 9); when I was weak, then I was strong (2 Cor 12 v 10). What he was preaching was nothing else but the foolish impotence of Christ crucified (1 Cor 1 & 2). But all that made sense for him, and makes sense for us, only if the overall orientation of our lives is the kingdom of God. To suffer on behalf of a kingdom other than God's, to be persecuted in the pursuit of our own interests or the defence of our own security is not redemptive suffering, however high minded we might be in it. It was only in the context of the kingdom that Jesus said: blessed are you who are persecuted, blessed are you when they speak evil about you, blessed are you poor.

Perhaps that is why we must be cautious of any facile language about 'the will of God' in times of catastrophe, or crisis, or serious illness. When people experience life as falling apart or caving in, they can only draw on their existing wisdom and perception. It is not a time for new understanding. Those who have come to know something of the kingdom in their daily lives, who have learnt the gift of self, and that all life is undeserved bonus, can transcend catastrophe sensing in it the redemptive hand of God. But those who have not, whose lives are turned in and who are trapped in an endless game of what is owed to them, cannot but experience catastrophe with resentment. To speak, in their case, of 'the will of God' is to compound their bitterness and strengthen their pagan ideas of 'God'.

The most that anyone who ministers God in such times of crisis can do is to help people recall what they already know. I felt this very keenly as a hospital chaplain at Warrington, but it also applies in the wider context of social or national catastrophe. Jesus' preaching, especially towards the end, had an urgent note of warning about pending catastrophe, and he kept saying that unless people are awake and watchful in good times, when still eating and drinking, and buying and selling, planting and building, then all will collapse, unredeemed, in time of crisis.

What I am getting at is that just as holes in our lives take their meaning from the context provided by our life as a whole, and especially that hole we call death, so our ability to transcend catastrophe or crisis—or death—and allow it to become redemptive depends on the central orientation of our life in more normal times. Indeed, when we talk of 'suffering' as redemptive we use the word in its active sense—how we stand in affliction, *sub-ferre,* to underpin or support—not in its passive sense of the affliction itself.

In the supreme case of Christ's cross, death drew its meaning from his life. And to make sense of why he chose it freely and why it was the will of a loving Father—in other words to understand how his death was the final statement of the story his life had told—we need a deeper perception of the political and psychological processes, the fears and threatened securities, which led to the final confrontation and death.

A second danger of lifting Jesus' death and resurrection out of its context and keeping alive that memory in a nonhistorical way is that it produces an abstract theology.

This has blighted our western Christian mentality for centuries – perhaps all the time, off and on, since the advent of 'Christendom'. We have known many theologies of redemption and atonement, from the time of St. Anselm in the late eleventh century to Calvin in the sixteenth, and thereafter. But many have been attempts to say why and how the cross was redemptive in its own right, and that has inevitably led to a treatment of God as requiring satisfaction to be made, restitution to be paid, in order to appease God. It is possible that if the cross had been understood more fully within the story which gave it meaning, our theology would not have strayed so far from the language of the New Testament, nor have become so abstract.

As it is we have an academic, abstract theology, a prepacked kit which we wander through life with, trying to apply. If we cannot apply it, it somehow remains intact, and we get on with life at large devoid of theology.

Since the reformation Christian thinkers were so preoccupied with that type of academic theology that our modern industrial and technological society grew up largely under its own dynamic, leaving theology where it belonged, in its sacristy. So we inherited a pietistic spirituality and an abstract theology, beautiful in their own domains but having little serious to say about the processes and experiences of contemporary life except be good and say your prayers, everything else will look after itself.

In the last decade or so we have begun to recover a much fuller, holistic, appreciation of the inter-relation of faith and life-as-a-whole, and the role of theology in pondering on and articulating that faith as an interpretation, critique, and source of hope and life within the actual world in which we live.

3. Jesus and politics

Recent scriptural studies have uncovered for us the extent to which Jesus entered totally into the social and political and religious realities of his day. (The books I have found most helpful are Albert Nolan's *Jesus before Christianity,* John Howard Yoder's *The Politics of Jesus,* and John Sobrino's *Christology at the Crossroads.*) It was a politically conscious age and Jesus made political options because there is no other way to incarnate God within human realities. He also laid his finger on very practical current issues. What we call the sermon on the Mount, for instance, was not a call to private virtue, but to a way of living and relating in accordance with God being a Father whose compassion, fidelity and dominion are for the whole of life and for all people.

The Kingdom Jesus originally preached was an anticipation into the affairs of life today, here, of the great Shalom, the fulfilled Kingdom of justice and love; it was not simply a conversion of heart, however essential that was, but a conversion of life.

It was also a kingdom to be received as 'gift', as 'grace'—a fact which Jesus seems to have had singular difficulty in conveying even to his nearest and dearest. For the Kingdom to be incarnated within human affairs and yet to be received wholly as gift is a dilemma which cannot yield to rational explanation. It can only be intuited in the dialectic and tension of intimate, persevering prayer on the one hand, and passionate involvement with people on the other. It is the experience of this tense and ambiguous dialectic which alone makes possible a living awareness both of God's total dominion and fatherhood, and also the absolute necessity of taking people seriously—with all that means in social awareness, political option, being a voice for the voiceless, and unmasking the falsities inherent in contemporary attitudes and language.

One senses a growing solitude in Jesus as the story proceeds. It was only the other day I noticed that sentence in Luke: 'Jesus was praying alone among his disciples when he said: "Who do people say I am?"' Picture the scene. Him. Them. His prayer. His aloneness. His need of them.

As the last confrontation approached, one feels his solitude mingled with a great sense of urgency: the fire in his belly and the absolute issues at stake; still misunderstood, even by his own apostles; time running out, and James and John still asking pathetic questions about having seats in his cabinet when the new regime takes over. What does one do when ultimate issues about God and people are burning in a solitude which cannot be conveyed and there is no time left?

'I have longed to eat this Passover Meal with you'. He left them, in the form of myth-action, what could not be left in words. 'This my body'. 'This my blood'. Do it to keep alive my memory, to make real where you are what has been and is real for me. The action will keep alive what you will never put in words; it will be a challenge to you to realize what I have realized, to live and die for what I have lived, and will die, for.

Jesus was killed for blasphemy and for political subversion. He had dared to bring together the implications of the holiness of God and the experienced realities of people's lives, and had dared, in the name of truth and love, to unmask the illusions and lies not only of the political/social order but also of the religious order. The cross leaves a permanent question mark behind any religious pre-conception of God, as well as any human social order.

When we make anamnesis, renewing the memory and realising the presence of Jesus, in his body and his blood, we celebrate a death and resurrection which took their meaning from the incarnation of the Word in the historical realities of his people. We thereby open and commit ourselves to the equivalent historical realities of our own day, our own people.

This is not, of course, to be reduced to fundamentalism. Jesus did not call everyone to follow him as apostles or prophets. But it does provide the central orientation for the Church as a whole, and for any local community of Christians. And it provides essential criteria for each of us in seeking to be faithful and obedient wherever we are in life.

4. The love of God is compassion for others

When we talk about the sun, we normally talk about its mediated effects as we experience them. And we do not need constantly to qualify our language because we all know that we can't talk about, or experience, the sun directly, only as mediated for us by the atmosphere.

The sun sets, the sun comes out, goes behind clouds. Look at the sun on that field. And so on.

Our language and ideas about God likewise do not make contact with God in himself. He is beyond our ken. But they do meet him in his mediated revelation and his effects within our experience.

That is why Christian tradition needs both the way of *affirmation,* talk about God and his ways, and also the way of *denial,* that no talk gives access to God in himself (which is possible only in the experience of the heart, not the head). All is of God, but nothing is God.

In scripture I think the unknowability of God was closely linked to the demands of justice and compassion. To love the Lord was not so much to feel an intensity of affective love for him, as to correspond with his compassion and love in the affairs of life.

Our belief in the holiness of God and the quality of our social awareness and love are two aspects of the same thing; they are not mutually independent realms.

For the Jews to adopt monotheism, for instance, was not a piece of abstract theology or self-contained liturgy. For God to be One was a radical social commitment to his people being one, over against the polytheism of contemporary pagans who had a god for the king, a god for the wealthy, a god for the powerless-... just as we have a Christ of bourgeois security and a Christ of the socially insecure and dispossessed—or, more starkly, a Christ of fascist juntas and a Christ of the church of the poor.

The God whom we worship is not other than the God with whom we correspond in the affairs of life. I think that is why Jesus so seldom (if at all) spoke of 'loving God' as a commandment, and did not seem to adopt the two commandments in his preaching. The 'economy' of the New Covenant was not you have two jobs to do, to love and worship God, and to love your neighbour. It was, rather, experience deeply and fully God's love and compassion for you and every person, then do likewise. As the Father has loved me, and I have loved you, so . . .

The sacred and the secular are interwoven in the whole of life. The contemplative and the social front liner understand each other more intimately than either is understood by one trapped in religiosity, who has God buttoned up in a religious system and ignores people.

The integration of sacred and secular, of liturgy and life, came home to me cruelly one day when I had been asked to celebrate Mass for a group on Family Fast Day. Between being asked and the actual time of the Mass I came to realise that nothing else in the group's life was facing up to being brothers and sisters of people dying of hunger, and that we were about to use the Eucharist as a substitute for, not a sacrament of, the gift of ourselves. I found the question crucifying, but in the end someone else had to take my place.

5. Communion in Christ

Many people think of Christianity thus: God is a spectator (slightly anxious); Jesus is a moral teacher; Christians are called to behave well, if rather unrealistically, in a naughty but 'real' world. God watches, and rewards them, they hope, if they pull it off O.K. Their prayer is largely an attempt to manipulate a fairly reluctant God into taking their 'real' world more seriously.

But Christian faith is in fact about accepting a radically new regime, a new order, brought about in Christ and being realised by his Spirit. It is somewhat like getting up one morning and opening a letter to say that a relative has died and, for various legal reasons, we have not only inherited another house but that the house we have lived in for decades no longer belongs to us. Everything around us goes on looking the same, but is in reality quite different; we have to learn quite new arts of how to live fully while no longer belonging, to live among familiar symbols claiming reality when we know them to be illusions, to work and eat and live and take life and one another seriously while at the same time knowing that all is passing away.

Christian behaviour is not the following of a new moral code introduced by Jesus; it is bringing daily life into accord with a new order of reality, that 'new creation' spoken of by Paul.

When Paul wrote to the Christians at Corinth about their bad behaviour while gathered for the Lord's supper, he did not say: you have been given a new command to treat each other as equals; you are not doing so, and God will not bless you. His argument was as follows: the Lord has brought about a new regime in Christ, a new communion established in the breaking of bread and the outpouring of wine; how can you still be living in a regime of dividedness? You are living a lie, which leads to damnation, if you communicate in the body and blood of Christ without 'discerning the body' which is his people. If God has established as gift a real order in which all people matter and are in communion, how can you carry on in the illusions (however plausible and seemingly human and real) of being divided, of dominating and disparaging one another?

The kingdom is not something which God is waiting around for us to bring off for him; it is gift, which God established and is realising by the power of his Spirit. His urging is not for us to achieve by moral endeavour what he has told us about, but to conform our lives to reality.

That is why, when we become aware of the marginal and dispossessed in our world—be they oppressed or starving brothers and sisters overseas, or emotionally and spiritually dispossessed here at home—when we become aware of them as kith and kin and struggle, however ambiguously, to conform our lives in keeping with that awareness, we are not setting up a communion previously absent. We are discovering a communion which pre-existed our awareness and response. We are moving out of the illusions and lies of bourgeois, class or nationalist attitudes and responses into reality, into truth. And that truth sets us free.

I think that is one reason why our communion in Christ with the dispossessed is a fundamental reality in all our lives wherever we are, and does not belong only to the front line activists, those immediately involved. No one who breaks the bread and pours the wine can evade being in that communion, and in many ways it is more crucifying for those at one (or several) removes from the front line, especially if they are influential or converse in the halls of power.

6. Being present and being effective

In any age there are ways of thinking which run so deep as to be unrecognised as peculiar to the age. One such, in our age, is our tendency to assess and value any action or decision by its effectiveness. It is called 'functionalism'. In its stark form, which we would all repudiate, it argues that nothing is valuable apart from its function, nothing worthwhile unless proved effective. It is a characteristic of scientific and technological thinking.

In its more subtle forms I suspect it colours our mental attitudes far more deeply than we know. We tend to recognise the vocation of the doctor or nurse but not of the patient, the vocation of the social worker but not of the afflicted, the role of the rich world but not of the poor (except as objects for development by the rich). Even phrases like 'the caring church' are tinged with our current need to justify ourselves by good works.

Yet for all our functionalism, we celebrate as the supremely salvific and liberating moment of history the hour when the Son of God was pinned powerless and crudely displayed as ineffective on the cross.

Christians talk today a great deal about mission, and in some quarters this is equated with bearing visible fruit and even success. But the Church's mission is to evangelise and to evangelise is not simply, or primarily, to bring in new members or to enliven old ones. To evangelise is to bring the good news of God into any area of life which is resistant or neutral. It includes the prophetic role of uncovering the dark areas of life, and the contemplative role of being present and poised to reality, with no tangible role or function.

There is a fundamentalist danger, which goes happily with functionalism, of equating the mission of the Church with that of the apostles. But neither Jesus nor the early Christians thought that was the only way to 'follow Jesus'. One only has to ponder the place of Mary, or other women and men in the gospels, to be cagey of any one-dimensional idea of mission. Many parts, one body. The eye cannot say to the hand 'I have no need of you' . . . The parts which seem to be weaker are indispensable (1 Cor 12).

We need that holistic appreciation of the body as a whole, and to recognise that for most people in most of their lives their mission is to bring the whole of life under the interpretation of faith. In other words a holistic understanding of all aspects of life as being relevant.

I have become increasingly suspicious in recent years of phrases about 'spiritual renewal' as if we can somehow become spiritual persons internally apart from decisions about behaviour.

When I was a young monk we used to say that being vowed to a life according to the rule of St. Benedict meant extracting from the rule (primarily its first eight chapters) the spirit of St. Benedict, virtues of humility and obedience and fidelity and silence. We read the remaining parts of the rule, largely to do with practical issues, with historical detachment.

But we have now come to realise that for Benedict such a distinction between the 'spiritual' and the 'practical' was meaningless. He was talking about a way of life, an incarnated way of life, in which practical decisions and behaviour are as necessary for 'running freely in the way of the Lord' as are inner attitudes. In fact both depend on each other. It would not, for instance, have occurred to him that a monk could have a spirit of detachment without in practice managing with a minimum and using all things with reverence and as communal. A craft did not give glory to God simply by intending it to, but by taking care of practical decisions such as what is charged for the produce. A monk could not become humble apart from behaving with humility. And so on. A holistic approach both to communal life and personal maturity which is more reminiscent of the Hebrew understanding of the person is necessary, a whole whose significance lies in its relationships, rather than our dualistic understanding of the self, autonomous and subdivided.

There is a great need to recover an incarnated wholeness, to re-learn to evangelise the neutral areas of life and experience, to work together in families, communities, parishes, wherever, to theologise what we have been conditioned to ignore. What is work? How do we decide about it? What does it mean to own money and other things? What does it mean to consume the earth's resources at the rate we do and with the violent techniques of agribusiness now established? How do we learn to savour the basic processes of life, the daily round, when all pressures are to disdain them? . . .

We cannot be a sacrament, a sign, of God's kingdom in the world, by spiritual renewal.

4. Fatalism and hope

The last reflection I share with you refers to the deep fatalism that is current today. Our sense of being the instruments, even play things, of political and economic processes which are beyond anyone's control. The objects of decisions made by smaller and smaller, more and more powerful, and ever more distant, moguls with no real answerability.

I think of the relentless pursuits of international capitalism – decisions initiated in lush board rooms in London or New York or Zurich and ending in blood in the villages and torture in the prisons of countries whose governments have less concern for their own people than for their economic security in the international game. I think of the demonic production of nuclear weapons, of the increasing production and sale of arms treated simply as lucrative trade. I think of the monetarist policies which elevate finance to an absolute – man for money, not money for man. I think of the pervasive, debilitating influence of commercial advertising, and I watch housewives shopping for over-processed, over-packed, tantalising goodies. And a dread comes over me. Who can set us free, not released into some subjective special escape world where we feel O.K., but free within and confronting these structural, demonic powers?

The good news which Jesus preached and activated so ambiguously among very ordinary and harassed people related to the arts of practical living within the dominating powers they experienced. He even had the absurdity to warn poor people not to hoard and store up things, and if in debt to get out of debt even if it cost them their last cloak or coat. In other words, it was essential to learn how to live free and poor whatever the pressures.

So there were two ways in which fatalism had to be countered. The art of living free within dominating powers, as well as the need to unmask and confront those powers. Both were needed, and in fact depended on one another. The former provided the platform which authenticated the latter; the latter provided the political realism which prevented the former becoming an irrelevant clique of the holy.

One of the remarkable facts of the early Church

was the short time it took for the Jesus who ended in disaster on the cross and in whose resurrection the apostles had initially failed to believe, for that same Jesus to be perceived as the source of authentic hope for all people, the true likeness of an unseen God broken into human history.

In the light of Christ's resurrection the early Christians came up with the same two responses to wordly powers and the danger of fatalism. They sought to live freely within the system (however ambiguous and equivocal their attempts) and they sought to unmask the powers that be.

Paul had the audacity, writing to the Christians at Collossae, to tell them that they had come alive, been re-born, in a Christ who was head of every Sovereignty and Power; indeed, that in the cross of Christ God had disarmed the Sovereignties and Powers, making a public spectacle of them.

Quite what Paul had in mind when speaking of Thrones, Dominations, Sovereignties and Powers has been much debated. Elemental powers which govern the world, certainly, and for him such powers had angelic or demonic connotations. But he was surely not talking about unearthly angels. By the end of the fourth century Dionysius had decided—since there had to be three threesomes of angels—that they must rank among these angelic choirs to make up the number. (A footnote in the Jerusalem Bible also refers to them simply as angels.) Is that not part of the spiritualising process which so often extracts Christian faith from political, incarnated realism? (Though, to be fair, angels were seen as very much involved in human affairs.)

It seems more likely that Paul is talking about what

the words actually say, that is the forms of wordly authority which claim dominion over people's lives. Christians under the Roman Empire knew as much about such things as we do today, the terrible power of structures and of political/economic language to tell people who they are, where they belong and what they are capable of doing and becoming.

I think Paul's claim is that the cross shows up as false this claim to dominion. At the point where secular authority and religious authority had combined to preserve national security by displaying Jesus as obviously absurd and powerless—at that point God had turned their wisdom into foolishness, and shown up their plausible claims as hot air. We would call it, today, 'de-mystification'.

Paul was not inciting people to anarchy, except in the noblest sense of that word. He was inviting Christians to discover themselves as people and to relativise all the powers and language which claim dominion or absolute interpretation of life.

In our own age today fatalism is not simply the result of the monolithic nature of structures of power (our thrones, dominations, powers) but also the fact that their economic and industrial language, and often their political language too, so limits the interpretation of what it is to be a person that people cannot believe in themselves. Their self-image is so cramped as to have no opening to the infinite realms of God. If one is no more than an economic unit, a work-hand, a goodies-consumer, a case for bureaucracy to deal with, there can be no hope. One is doomed to fear, boredom and fate.

Celebrating the body and blood of the Lord is not celebrating the glory of God over against, even at the expense of, the glory of man. Our faith is not about God being all and man being nothing. It is about God being man, and man being God.

So I often ponder, in the quietness of our small chapel, the enormous gap between the self-image of families living in our local housing estate (where the authorities lumped together 250 one-parent families) or in Toxteth, with the self-image spoken of by the Fathers of the Church and many of the mystics. What can bridge that gap?

> To this end alone were we created and do we live: to be like God; for we were created in his image.
>
> There is (first) a likeness to God which is only lost with life itself . . . it is there whether accepted or refused, both in one who can conceive it as in one who, foolishly, cannot . . . it derives from nature and not from will or endeavour.
>
> There is a second likeness, closer to God, in being freely willed. It lies in habits of life and inspires the soul to imitate the goodness of Supreme Good by its own virtue and his unchangeable eternity by its unflagging perserverance.
>
> But there is also a third likeness . . . so close in resemblance as to be called not simply likeness but unity of spirit. It makes man one with God, one spirit – not merely united in willing the same thing but in . . . being unable to will anything else.
>
> This is called unity of spirit not only because it is brought about by the Holy Spirit, who inclines one's spirit to it, but because it is itself the Holy Spirit, the God who is Charity. He who is the Love of Father and Son – their Unity, Sweetness, Good, Kiss, Embrace, and whatever else they share in that

supreme unity of truth and truth of unity—that Spirit becomes for man in regard to God (in the manner appropriate to man) what he is for the Son in regard to the Father or for the Father in regard to the Son (through their unity of being).

The soul in its happiness finds itself poised midway in the Embrace, the Kiss, of Father and Son. In a way beyond description and thought, the man of God is found worthy to become not God, but what God is; that is, man becomes through grace what God is through nature [William of St. Thierry, *The Golden Epistle,* Bk II, Chap. XVI].

CHAPTER EIGHT

'Because You Say "We See" . . .': Concerning ideology and sin

WHEN I was thirteen our religious knowledge master explained to us that the gravity of sin depended on three things. It depended on how Serious was the matter, how much one Intended to do it, and how much one knew what one was doing. And we could remember that, as I still do, don't I, by the letters S.I.N. (a slight wobble allowed on the third one).

That was, for the time being, excellent instruction and I still remember joining in suggested examples to illustrate each element. If one stole half a crown from someone who had money it could not be gravely sinful because the matter was not serious enough really to engage one's whole person—but what about stealing ten pounds or stealing half a crown from someone who was poor?

It was not nit-picking casuistry but, at that age, a wise release from a lurking fear of falling into serious sin all over the place (in fact one could not fall into sin, only jump, want to be pushed, or slide: that was the I bit and the N bit).

After five more school years and two more in the navy, I found myself as a novice beginning to get to know the psalms. And as time went on it dawned on me that the psalmist, like the prophets, had a different idea about sin and sinners. The 'wicked', the 'sinners', the 'fools', were not those who worked evil in the world knowingly but those who worked evil, oppressed others, were pompous and go-getting as a social fact. It didn't seem to matter much whether or not they knew what they were doing, whether they felt guilty or not. If anything, their ignorance and lack of answerability made things worse for them, not better—at least as the psalmist saw things.

Later on another doubt assailed my childhood S.I.N.. In the gospels Jesus seemed to manage much better among people who did not behave very well than he did among those who behaved impeccably. Maybe what he was on about was not simply to get people to behave well? Maybe the good news in Jesus Christ was something much more than ethics and moral virtue? Maybe there is a good beyond the ethical good, and an evil beyond the ethical bad? Maybe Mary of Magdala did have something which Simon the pharisee had missed?

And finally I found myself wondering why, on a number of occasions in the gospels, those who are sick or afflicted are assumed also to be in sin. At first I thought that it was a long out-dated primitive way of thinking—to assume that material or mental affliction was a curse from God and must be the outcome of sin.

Wasn't the whole book of Job trying to get away from that infantile attitude?

But then in unguarded moments I caught myself thinking like that. I'd meet someone afflicted in some way and find myself, almost subconsciously, saying 'of course if they pulled themselves together . . . ' or 'if they were more like me . . . '. It was a defence mechanism deep in my psyche in the presence of a really wounded brother or sister, a technique for keeping my own self image intact, of distancing myself from their woundedness which would otherwise have to be mine also.

For years these thoughts floated around in my head and my heart, and only recently—as is the way if we live with ambiguities long enough—some light dawned while pondering chapter 9 in John's gospel, his beautiful and wittily told story of the man born blind. Read it if you can, before we go on.

The story unfolds thus:

1. Jesus covers the man's eyes with a poultice and sends him to recover his sight in the pool. (As usual Jesus demands an action of faith to enable the cure.)
2. The man is summoned to the authorities, some of whom can see nothing in Jesus' action except that it should not have been done on the Sabbath.
3. The man's parents are summoned, but dodge getting involved in the issue.
4. The authorities again summon the man, who by this time has discovered a freedom and vigour that must have amazed even himself. At one point he taunts them by asking why are you so fascinated by Jesus? Are you going to join him?

(A little bit like someone asking a Minister of Defence why are you so fascinated by C.N.D.? Are you signing on?) They eventually drive him out, saying that he is a sinner through and through, because of his blindness since birth.

5. Jesus goes in search of the man, who until then had never seen Jesus. And a typically Johannine dialogue ensues, each phrase reflecting our own call to faith:

   Do you believe in the Son of Man?
   Tell me who he is.
   You are looking at him and he is speaking to you.
   I do believe.

Now this story is told by John between an opening and a closing question and answer. They are crucial to the story:

Q. Did this man or his parents sin that he should be born blind?
A. Neither he nor his parents sinned.
Q. (the authorities) We are not blind surely?
A. Since you say 'We see' your guilt remains.

These opening and closing brackets to the story highlight its central theme—that in the actions of Jesus the accepted norms of who is O.K. and who is not O.K. are reversed; i.e. he becomes a judgement on accepted norms. 'It is for judgement that I have come . . . so that those without sight may see and those with sight turn blind'.

In order to grasp in a more contemporary way what was going on in John chapter 9 it may be easiest to reflect on our modern understanding of *ideology*.

The word was coined at the beginning of the last century by a French philosopher, and has been used in a variety of ways since then. Marx, for instance, used it to support his thesis that all our ideas are socially conditioned by class structures. Others have used *ideology* to describe that set of ideas we have to interpret life but which in fact cover for our emotional insecurity. Ideology defines what is true, for our own interests, and prevents us perceiving truth in a disinterested, maybe threatening, way.

Today the word is used either in a *neutral* sense to describe that set of ideas or symbols which each of us has to enable us to understand ourselves and what is going on in our world, or it is used in a *pejorative* sense to refer to a dominant ideology in society—dominant in that it belongs to a certain set of people who make their ideology normative for everyone else, and dominant also in that ideas embedded in the ideology are more important than the people and events they are seeking to understand.

In Jesus' day the dominant ideology was the Law. In our day the dominant ideologies are Russian-style Marxism; Western-individualist-capitalism, when legitimised by theories of the New Right, or baptised by Born Again Christian moralism; Islamic Fundamentalism.

Christian faith is not in itself an ideology, being centred in a person rather than a set of ideas—though Christians have been, and are, adept at reducing it to an ideology. (Apparently Dubcek was encouraged to embark on his liberalising of communism in Czechoslovakia by meeting Catholic student friends at university and realising how the Church was seeking to recover its authentic faith and life from the grip of ideology.)

There are common characteristics in dominant ideologies. And to clarify these may help us to appreciate both what Jesus was confronting in his day, and also clarify where our confrontations should lie today.

1) An ideology is born out of *high minded, well-intentioned* and often long cherished thinking.

   The Law, in itself, was a beautiful portrayal of how human affairs should mirror the affairs of God.

   Western individualism, in so far as it seeks to express the unique dignity and freedom of every person, can hardly be questioned.

   Marx's insight into the political and economic interdependence of different classes was a re-emergence of what everyone claims to believe: that we are members one of another.

   Ideologies are plausible, mentally attractive, even addictive, because they are born of high-minded truth.

2) Ideology reduces the fulness of life *to limited criteria.*

   The language of an ideology is limited to certain criteria, goes round and round within those limited criteria and becomes ever more competent within its own tunnel. In so doing it forces life into its own mould, so that instead of thought enabling us to understand experience and life, it dominates them.

   The law was made for man, not man for the law. Again and again in the Gospels and in St.

Paul one hears that cardinal message of freedom: that the Law cannot deliver, of itself, that which the Law is all about.

We live in an equally reductionist age. For the sake of coherence life is reduced to politics, politics to economics, economics to finances. Man is made for cash, not cash for man. And anyone who questions that is assumed to be a dreamer with feet a mile off the ground.

3) Because the language and vision is tunnelled, ideology is able to be extremely *forthright and persuasive.* Just as there is a forthrightness that comes from breadth of vision, love of truth and unconcern for self, so there is a forthrightness that comes from narrowness of vision, a love of being right, and a concern for self. The latter is especially dangerous when people at large feel lost or fearful. It becomes highly persuasive because people long to be in the secure hands of people who are sure of themselves.

4) *For those who subscribe* to a dominant ideology, it provides a total rationalisation for their own righteous self-image. It relieves them of any moral guilt, any sense of being counted among the sinners.

There is, of course, in all of us a deep desire to keep our self-image intact. We use all sorts of defence mechanisms to remain whole and complete in our own eyes (and hopefully in the eyes of others). Even before God, I, Thomas, try to remain upright, treating him as a partner who is lucky to have me around; 'I am Thomas, Lord; who are you?'

This intactness is superbly retained by high-minded ideas about law keeping and good behaviour (the occupational hazard of scribes and pharisees); it is superbly retained by fundamentalist and moralistic forms of Christian faith. Yet it is precisely that desire to keep ourselves whole and O.K. which has to be abandoned, has to be humbled, before we can be set free to perceive and pursue reality—what is really happening to people—even if it shatters our public and private 'persona'.

5) *Those who cannot or choose not to subscribe* are, conversely, set up not only as misfits but as guilty. As often as not this makes *victims into culprits.*

In Jesus' time it was in fact impossible for any but a few to be educated enough to know the law and have sufficient freedom to keep it. Most people were not only second class but seen to be under a sort of curse. This was especially true of those whose disabilities could be clearly named, the lepers, the blind, the mentally sick, or whose home region as a whole made them despised as not being the real thing, the Galileans for instance. All these were somehow 'accursed and outside the law', 'in sin from birth'.

Our present equivalents are no less vicious, even if we are careful not to admit them. In a dominant regime which values self-improvement, getting on in the world, and competition as the only evidence of loyalty, those who cannot cope or choose not to are set up as misfits and guilty. There is an unvoiced assumption that those who cannot find work could do so if they tried harder or were more 'like us'. Recent shifts in housing regulations imply that our thousands of homeless families could in fact find homes if they tried harder. The constant reference to inflation being caused by excessive wage demands creates the impression that wage earners are the disloyal wreckers, leaving those on salaries (maybe complete with expense accounts and company cars) as loyal and innocent.

The victims become the culprits.

For Jesus such victimisation was abhorrent. It was not that he subscribed to a contemporary version of what a friend of mine calls 'the assumption that everything working class is good and middle class is bad'. I don't think Jesus subscribed to any simplistic ideas that any group as such was morally innocent. But he was adamant that the Father is the ulitimate source of life for all people and that to divide them into the just and the unjust (which ideology always does) fails to acknowledge that God's sun and rain (the ultimate sources of life) fall on the fits and misfits and unfits alike. All are dependent.

When Paul says that Jesus was 'made sin', or the gospels reflect on how he took our sins on himself, and was counted among the sinners and outcasts, are they not referring to his option for, and being counted among, the victims-seen-as-culprits? And what are the social and theological implications of that for those who seek to follow him?

6) *Those who cannot make it* are not only seen to be, *but see themselves to be guilty.*

Because a dominant ideology sets a norm to which all people are expected to aspire, those who cannot do so come to see themselves as inadequate, somchow accursed, somehow under a bondage of sin.

When Jesus heals the man in John's story he liberates him from far more than blindness. The man discovers himself to have a place in the world for the first time ever. And at the same time he discovers God to be one who sets him free from that fatalistic bondage and empowers him with amazing confidence: he is not the God who imposes fate. Jesus spent much of his time calling those with a deflated self-image to enter life and history through faith and fearlessness, and those with an inflated self-image to enter life and history through a wholesome fear of God and awareness of their common humanity.

In our own society the dominant culture presents a high standard of material well-being, aided by every latest fashion from clothing to electronic devices as mandatory on everyone. And it is the very nature of advertising to present as mandatory and normative that which is just beyond the experience and reach of most people. The result is a permanent sense of being inadequate, of never quite making it, of being under a sort of curse, never quite to belong. In a local housing estate the word gets round among teenagers that to be 'in' this season one must have the latest design in Italian trainer shoes. In order to cope, Mum has three part time jobs to raise the cash to buy off her teenage son with said trainers—to buy him off partly because she is out of the house so much. We speak of freedom, but the psychological pressures and control mechanisms on people are immense, while all the time being presented as freedom.

We cannot, of course, destroy such domination, but as fools for Christ's sake it is surely possible to dance free, to live cheerfully by alternatives, to laugh at the moral seriousness of the ideology, to evolve bit by bit, and in detail, a consumer asceticism, to discover the joy of being at home to ourselves, at home to people and at home to God.

7) *'Who is not for us is against us'.*

A dominant ideology, because it claims to understand the totality of life and have solutions to everything, becomes a false God. It becomes an idol making that claim which God alone can make: I will be faithful to my promises.

The psalmist laughs at such totalitarian claims. Idols, he says, have eyes but cannot see, have ears but cannot hear, have hands but cannot feel. They claim omnipotence, look like the real thing but in the end cannot deliver the life they promise.

But this totalitarian tendency also inevitably sets up the world scene as a two-adversary confrontation. There is no room for third parties. The whole issue of history and salvation is presented as the struggle between angels of light and angels of dark, the good and the evil, a social version of the ancient and insidious Manichaean heresy, an ultimate denial of the heart of scriptural faith which will not accept the issue of personal or social history as that between a part of creation which is all good and another part all bad. God created all good, but in its historical reality all is good-yet-disordered-and-fallen. Nothing, and no-one, is beyond redemption nor free from the need of redemption.

A dominant ideology, because it is self-righteous, cannot accept this; it can only accept a two-party, good-evil confrontation. Any third party must be in fact and perhaps unwittingly a tool of the opposite side. Any criticism is subversion, any seeking of alternatives is disloyalty. C.N.D. must be a plaything of the Kremlin. Nicaragua can in no way be a third alternative (by definition there is no third alternative). National security is absolute, and anyone who questions that must be a traitor. Ah! Jerusalem, Jerusalem, if only you had known the way that is for your peace. But you still murder the prophets . . . In the face of absolute issues and absolute security it is obvious that one man, ten thousand, six million, should die for the sake of the people.

8) A dominant ideology is *inherently violent and needs an enemy.*

In our monastic life we often find that intellectually gifted people have a tendency to live so much in a world of ideas that they evade, or at least postpone, getting into contact with their own emotional and intuitive selves, and they tend to deny their own dark space within. Living thus by ideas rather than reality they also tend to be aggressive, judgmental and defensive. Other people become either the victims or the enemies of their own mind-set of ideas.

High-minded ideas provide the best security for one's own in-tact-ness and the projection onto others of the dark areas ignored in oneself. (A little bit of autobiography!)

At the wider level of dominant ideologies in society the same process operates. It is not only the two paranoid bullies, the U.S. Administration and the Kremlin, who need each other as nameable enemies and who ironically become mirror images to one another. All nations which are dominated by a single forthright ideology must have enemies. It is in fact their enemies who define their own self-image, and allow them to ignore their own failure and darkness.

9) Finally, a dominant ideology, being more concerned to *prove itself right* (to itself and to the world) than to perceive truth, *perverts language to its own ends.*

It is worth pondering seriously how it was that the authorities, in John's story, when presented with the self-evident truth of a man being released from blindness, could see in that nothing but the fact that it broke the Sabbath law and was done by the wrong person. We meet so many parallel cases today—the inability to see anything as good, anything as life-giving, if it comes from the wrong camp.

I think this is more to do with sophisticated blindness than simple malice. It is not that the action of the other camp is seen as good and then carefully re-interpreted (though that of

> course happens). It is rather that an ideology so dominates the interpretation of what is possible that the other camp is incapable of goodness or truth. It is only capable, by definition, of P.R. stunts, political manipulation, bad will.
>
> When ideas thus dominate reality, language becomes their plaything. The USSR has evolved a whole philosophy of the use of language as support for its ideology and not as communication of truth. But the same perversion happens in our own countries. I think of the way the word 'communist' is used, even by Catholics who delight to celebrate saints who today would all be called subversive communists.
>
> And by what process of righteous thinking can anyone come to the point of saying, in the name of Christianity: we can only be peace makers from a position of power? Is that not the ultimate denial of the Cross?

Where, then, does such a survey of the demonic powers of ideology leave us? Perhaps if we could understand more clearly what ideologies do to people, and especially how they cast the vast majority of people, the poor, into being dispossessed and fated outcasts, then we could appreciate what liberation and hope Jesus was living for and also what we can live for today. Is it not along these lines – and not along moralistic lines – that we should see Jesus as being 'counted among the sinners', that we should understand 'Lamb of God who takes sin away'?

It would help us appreciate why Jesus' good news seemed so ambiguous to many of his contemporaries, even his own followers. And it would help us to cope with similar misunderstanding and ambiguity in our day. It would, of course, be a good news that divides the hearts of many, a good news that would confront much that is accepted uncritically, a good news that would divide us even from our own people. But he did not come to bring a peace that never divides. To live the peace that *he gives* is to learn the art of being vagabonds, displaced persons, fools. Can we take it (and not be righteous ourselves!)?

As we ponder all these things in our hearts, as we pray the psalms (which speak of them all), as we re-read the gospels, as we seek to open ourselves to the great powers of death and evil in our contemporary world, as we sense that much of our privatised, spiritualised and moralised spirituality cannot interpret the scene we are in, and then as we begin to sense the futility of God and his kingdom and ourselves as part of that—what do we do? How do we cope?

One reaction is a yearning to set up an alternative and effective programme for God.

Shortly before John Paul II left Britain he was at a large youth rally in South Wales. As he boarded the helicopter to leave, he turned, opened his arms, and said, 'Young people, young people, build the kingdom, build the kingdom'.

That phrase is common enough today; it appears even in liturgical prayers. But my quizzical mind wondered at the time whether Jesus would ever have used it and if not, why not? And then I recalled that it was from near that same corner of Britain, by the river Severn, that a British monk had gone to Rome and told the loose-living Romans that they should get themselves organised, try harder, and save themselves. Was it perhaps his ghost which managed, at that last moment, to whisper into the Pope's ear: Build the Kingdom? The ghost of Pelagius having the last word!?

Certainly the Anglo-Saxons and Celts have never needed another heresy. That one has lasted for fifteen centuries.

The Kingdom: Jesus spoke of the kingdom being near at hand, among us, yet-to-be but here already. He told people they could, or could not, enter it, but never said they were in it. (Only one man was said to be 'not far from it'.) The kingdom was realised in history, yet was always more than history could expect; it was always experienced as gift and as grace, but was never magic. It demanded all the preparation and predisposition that gift-receiving does demand (the social justice required by the Year of the Lord's Favour), and yet the kingdom was never merited.

Like all love affairs, the kingdom was enigmatic, better talked of in stories and celebration than in books and theses. And like all love affairs it was recognised only by those who knew it by experience. You could know it but not know about it.

I have come to think that the main thrust of all Jesus' preaching was to persuade people to accept this antecedent reality of God's presence and creativity. It is the love of God in people's lives, his antecedent kingdom, which urges us. It is not the building of something on his behalf, this spectator-God, waiting for us to do great things in his name. This is beautifully expressed by a Masai elder speaking to Vincent Donovan in Tanzania:

> He said: 'For a man really to believe is like a lion going after its prey. His nose and eyes and ears pick up the prey. His legs give him the speed to

catch it. All the power of his body is involved in the terrible death leap and single blow to the neck with the front paw, the blow that actually kills. And as the animal goes down, the lion envelops it in his arms (Masai refer to the front legs of an animal as its arms), pulls it to himself, and makes it part of himself. This is the way a lion kills. This is the way a man believes. This is what faith is.'

I looked at the elder in silence and amazement. Faith understood like that would explain why, when my own faith was gone, I ached in every fibre of my being. But my wise old teacher was not finished yet.

'We did not search you out, Padri', he said to me. 'We did not even want you to come to us. You searched us out. You followed us away from your house into the bush, into the plains, into the steppes where our cattle are, into the hills where we take our cattle for water, into our villages, into our homes. You told us of the High God, how we must search for him, even leave our land and our people to find him. But we have not done this. We have not left our land. We have not searched for him. He has searched for us. He has searched us out and found us. All the time we think we are the lion. In the end the lion is God.'

The lion is God. Of course. Goodness and kindness and holiness and grace and divine presence and creating power and salvation were here before I got here. Even the fuller understanding of God's revelation to man, of the salvific act that had been accomplished once and for all for the human race, was here before I got here. My role as a

> herald of that gospel, as messenger of the news of what had already happened in the world, as the person whose task it was to point to 'the one who had stood in their midst whom they did not recognize' was only a small part of the mission of God to the world. It was a mysterious part; a demanded part: 'Woe to me if I do not preach the gospel.'
>
> It was a role that would require every talent and insight and skill and gift and strength I had, to be spent without question, without stint, and yet in the humbling knowledge that only that part of it would be made use of which fits into the immeasurably greater plan of the relentless, pursuing God whose will on the world will not be thwarted. The lion is God [Vincent Donovan in *Christianity Rediscovered,* Orbis Books, 1978].

When we first find ourselves 'hungering and thirsting for what is right', the chances are that we are more or less Pelagian and have a reasonably clear ideology. We set out 'to do God's will', and he is indeed lucky to have us around to do it. We the actors, he the spectator.

For some, that state of affairs lasts until middle age tempers it and they move sedately into mediocrity and compromise.

But what should happen, and I believe is the normal progress for Christians in any walk of life who have remained alert, seeking and prayerful, is a transition from being in dialogue with God as neighbour (with all the demarcation disputes involved in that) to being in union with God. The mystics talk much to us about this, but we should not think of it as proper to a privileged few. Mission in areas of conflict, or crises in life which remove any clarity about what we can or ought to do, imprisonment, the destruction of all we have given our lives for, serious illness, even being present to scenes of irrational violence (as in our riots in Liverpool five years ago)—all these moments are demands from God to step into quite a new type of presence and communion.

It is a conversion which we cannot programme or achieve, but which God's Spirit will work in us if we are open to it and persevering. We recognize it by hindsight. It is, I believe, the transition

- —from 'coming to do God's will' (Psalmist) to really seeking 'that God's will be done in us' (Mary)
- —from moral endeavour *for* God to contemplative union *with* him.

This conversion should, I think, happen in all our lives, this conversion from active endeavour to contemplative union. It may happen dramatically, or it may creep up on us softly, softly; but it is not an oddity for a mystical few. On the other hand it can easily be missed because it feels like a loss of certainty, a loss of faith, a leap into the dark. It is like a ship leaving the security of navigation lights and finding itself in open sea. There is need for mutual encouragement in this. When you are afraid of 'going round the bend', friends to go round the bend with are precious —or even guidance from those who have already gone round.

Five final thoughts to share with you:

1) *This conversion ushers in an intense solitude of communion.*

We discover that the heart of ourselves is not in the end an ultimate aloneness but a radical solidarity and communion with all God's beloved people.

This communion is a living conversation with the poor, the forgotten, the voiceless, the wounded, the dispossessed. So we carry in ourselves, wherever we are, a deep suffering (perhaps the social equivalent of that wound of love that St. Teresa and other mystics speak of). We bear wounds of love which never heal, the wounds of the risen Lord.

2) *But we also carry an intense joy,* because the Christian is not merely a striver for liberation yet to come but a bearer of a liberation of which the down-payment, the pledge, has already been made. It is an enigmatic co-existence of suffering and joy which makes our lives, especially our community lives, into living signs: it is a transition

—from being patrons of the Kingdom, to being instruments of the Kingdom (today we have a thousand patrons of peace to every one instrument of peace)

—from Jesus' initial 'follow me' to Peter by the lakeside calling him to work for and preach the kingdom, to his second 'follow me' by the lakeside after Peter had lost any self-assurance other than loving the Lord! 'When you were young you girded yourself and went where you would; but the time comes when you will be girded by others and not go where you choose. Follow me'. (*Domine, quo vadis?*)

3) *It is a conversion—from living out of duty* and thereby keeping our self-image intact, our autarchic ego respectable, to abandoning that entire game of 'being somebody' before God and others. It is the conversion which Paul talks of so often in Romans, and is beautifully worked out in Chapter 8; God's Spirit releases us from loving through moral endeavour, to being able to love freely, as it were, naturally.

   The conversion always involves a death; indeed, this side of the grave, it involves a constant dying, but only that a new life and freedom may be released in us. We learn what it is to constantly carry in the Body (our community of faith) the dying of Jesus so that his risen life may be manifest. And, surprise, surprise, this freedom from fear makes us invincible: you cannot kill me for I have died already. Or, as Paul sings at the end of that chapter, I am now sure that neither death nor life—no 'power'—can come between us and the love of God.

4) *But it is not a conversion from serious good-think to amateurish good will.*

   How do we remain tough-minded as well as being tender-hearted? The conversion I talk of is not to an anti-intellectual sentimentality, nor to an indifferent liberalism. There is no escape, for instance, from the need for serious social analysis, nor from what is now called contextual theology—the arduous task of taking the actual social realities we are in as the contemporary agenda for understanding the 'hope that is within us'.

   Ideology is intellectual idolatry and like most

idols is not coped with by smashing! If work is my idol I do not cope with it by laziness. If ideas are, I do not cope with it by sentimentalism.

I have mentioned Paul's autobiographic account in Romans. He had been trapped in the strong, all-embracing ideology of The Law, and had then had to face the humility of recognising that that ideology was incapable of delivering the very life of which it spoke. He came to see that intelligence without love is demonic, that single-mindedness without compassion deals death. And it is my belief that the criteria of love which he lists in 1 Corinthians 13 are his own autobiographic check-lists to discern whether or not our tough-mindedness is truly tender-hearted, whether we are seeking and loving truth or merely to be right. 1 Corinthians 13 asks all the crucial questions raised by the characteristics of ideology which I surveyed above. Why not have a go?

5) *Living in the present* — one final comment to end with: all our work and endeavour is surely, in the end, to enable the daily things of people's lives to give glory to God. It is the experience of a number of people I know that the conversion I have tried to speak of enables us to live far more fully in the present, and to savour all things.

'In practice the way to contemplation is an obscurity so obscure that it is no longer even dramatic. There is nothing left in it that can be grasped and cherished as heroic or even unusual —And so... there is a supreme value in the ordinary routine of work and poverty and hard-

> ship and monotony that characterise the lives of all the poor and uninteresting and forgotten people in the world' [Thomas Merton, in *Seeds of Contemplation*].

We are not really artisans in God's world, are we!? We are 'God's work of art' (Ephesians). All the time we think we are the lion. In the end, the lion is God!

CHAPTER NINE

A Homily

WHO is your God?

If he is Creator of All Things – then why has so much slipped through his hands?

If he is All Good – then why so much suffering and affliction?

If he is All Mighty – then why, oh why, does he not deliver the goods?

If my God is Almighty, All Good, Creator of All, then I am condemned to a continual game of bandying words with him, asking in as many clever ways as I can devise: Why do you not restore the fortunes of your people? And he will always disappoint me.

What is more, my involvement and work for Justice and for Peace will be 'on behalf of' an abstract, absent, spectating God. It will be more to do with moral fervour, self-justification, even religious loyalty, than the expression of lived faith in a passionate God.

The educated part of each of us seeks clever understanding. The 'religious' part seeks signs of God's power. But the heart of faith, in us, proclaims the Cross, this enigma of God's foolishness – so much wiser. Where are the clever debaters, the learned and scientific, the economists and politicians, of our day? Who can be clever, or indeed religious, before a God who dies for his people?

Inherited Illusions

The Cross, the Death of Christ, what did it mean? What does it say to us? What does it demand of us?

A person dies for what he lives for. Jesus died for taking a specific social, indeed political, stand in life. Blessed are you poor—the Kingdom of God is yours. The Christian, the Church, is called to the same stand and the same Cross.

It has often been said in recent years that the Church (you and me) must take a fundamental option for the poor. (It has recently been said again at Puebla.) But Christ calls to more than that. He does not say that the Church is *for* the poor, but the Church is *of* the poor. She is 'at home' only in the Kingdom, and the Kingdom is 'at home' only among the poor.

And this turns upside down all human sense and social norms. The margins know God, the centre knows him not.

If the Church is of the poor, then we who are privileged to serve are in the Church on sufferance. That is, salvation is mediated through the poor, the powerless, the afflicted—not the other way round. It is only the poor who can reveal, who can lay bare, the terrible hidden illusions and lies, so prettily embedded in polite bourgeois society.

So what for us who are bourgeois, who inherit, like it or not, middle class norms (and all who hear or read this are more or less middle class) and then find ourselves, not only confronted by the weary cry of the poor in our world, but also living in a society and among very good people utterly conformed and structured to the illusions of comfortable living?

We are in agony, a quite special agony, and one that questions almost everything in our 'given' life. It is my belief that this agony is 'crucial'. It must not be evaded; it must be allowed to crucify us (as far as possible without guilt and fearful anxiety—though who is free of those!?).

We are often encouraged to evade the agony:

1) Because there is *nothing we can do.* (Yes, we can attend meetings, write and read papers, dabble with lifestyle; but come now—there's nothing we can really do, consciously, to feed the hungry, clothe the naked ... in our modern world.) But God's supreme moment in the life of Christ was precisely when he could 'do' nothing—naked, impotent, absurd, on the Cross. It was that 'hour' and that alone which enabled resurrection and new life. It is far more basic to 'exist with' people than to 'act for' them. And the agony we experience, and must live, is our 'existing with' those in the margins, even while we live in the centre. Let no one say to you: don't bother about things you can do nothing about. Sooner or later God will use you to bear fruit, but the fruit will be real only to the extent that the pruning knife of agony has pruned you.

2) We also evade the agony *because so many good people see things quite other than ourselves.* Well of course they do. They did then, and always have. It has never really been an issue between good people and bad people. In fact, I'm beginning to suspect that until we experience ourselves as enigmatic to good people, it is probable that real faith has not yet taken hold of us. Until we find ourselves (however reluctantly) at odds

> with the good sense of normal society, aliens and strangers and misfits—until we find *that* happening, it is not really the Gospel that has taken us. The Kingdom does not really 'fit' anywhere.

So I say: Let the Agony crucify your life. It is *your* way of 'existing with' the afflicted of the world. Take the agony into your prayer, let it force practical decisions in your life. *Be* Justice and Peace in your life (in case *doing* Justice and Peace activities be so much conscience salving and self justifying).

And then you will be poised for God to use you in ways you can never plan or know beforehand. You will become instruments of *his* justice and *his* peace.

Table of Original Publication and Delivery

1. The Passion of Political Love—June 1981, to the A.G.M. of the Catholic Institute for International Relations (C.I.I.R.).
2. Violence Within and Violence Without—October 1979, at the Upholland Northern Institute.
3. Of Prayer and Praxis—May 1981, in *The Month.*
4. The Psalms and the Poor—April 1979, in the *Clergy Review.*
5. Eucharist and Politics—1974, as a C.I.I.R. pamphlet.
6. Hope and Expectation: How We Live the Story—1982, in *One for Christian Renewal.*
7. Reliving the Memory: Making Anamnesis—1982, to the Liverpool Ecumenical Clergy Conference.
8. 'Because You Say "We See" . . .': Concerning Ideology and Sin—1984.
9. A Homily—1980, to the Assembly of the Justice and Peace Commission.